CANADA
Invents

SUSAN HUGHES

Illustrations by Paul McCusker

Owl

Dedication

For my son, Kevin, and his pal Jake—whose energetic questions delight, exasperate, provoke, challenge, and enrich me—and all who have the joy of knowing them!

Owl Books are published by Maple Tree Press Inc.
51 Front Street East, Suite 200, Toronto, Ontario M5E 1B3

The Owl colophon is a trademark of Owl Children's Trust Inc.
Maple Tree Press Inc. is a licensed user of trademarks of Owl Children's Trust Inc.

Distributed in the United States by Firefly Books (U.S.) Inc.
230 Fifth Avenue, Suite 1607, New York, NY 10001

We acknowledge the financial support of the Canada Council for the Arts, the Ontario Arts Council, and the Government of Canada through the Book Publishing Industry Development Program (BPIDP) for our publishing activities.

Cataloguing in Publication Data

Hughes, Susan, 1960–
Canada invents

Includes index.
ISBN 1-894379-23-3 (bound)   ISBN 1-894379-24-1 (pbk.)

1. Inventions — Canada — Juvenile literature. 2. Inventors — Canada — Juvenile literature.
I. McCusker, Paul. II. Title.

T23.A1H83 2002   j609.71   C2001-930424-2

Design and art direction: Word and Image Design Studio
Illustrations: Paul McCusker

Printed in Hong Kong

A   B   C   D   E   F

CONTENTS

The World of Inventions   4

Snow and Ice: Inventions to Cope with Canada's Cold   9

Ka-boom!: Inventions of Energy and Power   21

Fun and Games: Inventions That Amuse and Entertain   31

"Hello? Is Anybody There?": Inventions That Communicate   43

Float, Sink, and Roll Along: Inventions on the Move   55

Up in the Air: Inventions That Fly   67

Digging In: Edible Inventions   77

Some Body: Inventions That Meet Physical Challenges   89

Bit and Pieces: A Mixed Bag of Inventions   99

Acknowledgements   110

Index   111

The World of Inventions

Inventions surround you. From the time you wake up in the morning until the time you go to bed at night, you are using inventions. The bed you sleep in and the sheets you fling off when you get up are inventions. So are the cereal you eat for breakfast and the spoon you eat it with. Your toothbrush, your toothpaste, and the sink you spit into. Yes, even the toilet! In fact, you can hardly turn around without bumping into an invention.

Televisions, swimming pools, telephones, cars, tree forts, and computers are all inventions. So are your clothes and books, the games you play, and even some of the food you eat. The process of making flour from wheat was an invention, and day-care centres, restaurants, and paid dog-walking services are too!

TESTING, TESTING, ONE ... TWO

So how can you tell what is an invention and what isn't? Try the one-two test.

1. An invention is something created by a person. It can be a thing, such as a skateboard or a squirt gun, but it doesn't have to be a product or something you can touch. An invention can also be a process. It can be a new way to do something, such as developing a way to freeze fish so it can be shipped and sold across the country.

2. An invention solves a problem in a new way. An invention like a car solves the problem "How can I get there without walking?" A game solves the problem "How can I have some fun?" An invention like a restaurant solves the problem "How can I get something to eat without having to cook it myself?"

Want to know if something is an invention? If in doubt, give it the old one-two test.

DISCOVERIES AND INNOVATIONS

A discovery is something noticed for the first time. Some very important discoveries have been made by Canadians. For example, Frederick Banting and Charles Best, an American colleague, discovered a hormone called insulin. Insulin was able to help people who were suffering from diabetes, a disease that, at the time, resulted in death. But discoveries aren't inventions, so you won't find any in this book.

An innovation, on the other hand, changes or improves an existing invention. In Canada, 90 per cent of patents are given out for innovations. In this book, you'll find examples of both innovations and inventions, but to keep it simple, we're calling them all inventions.

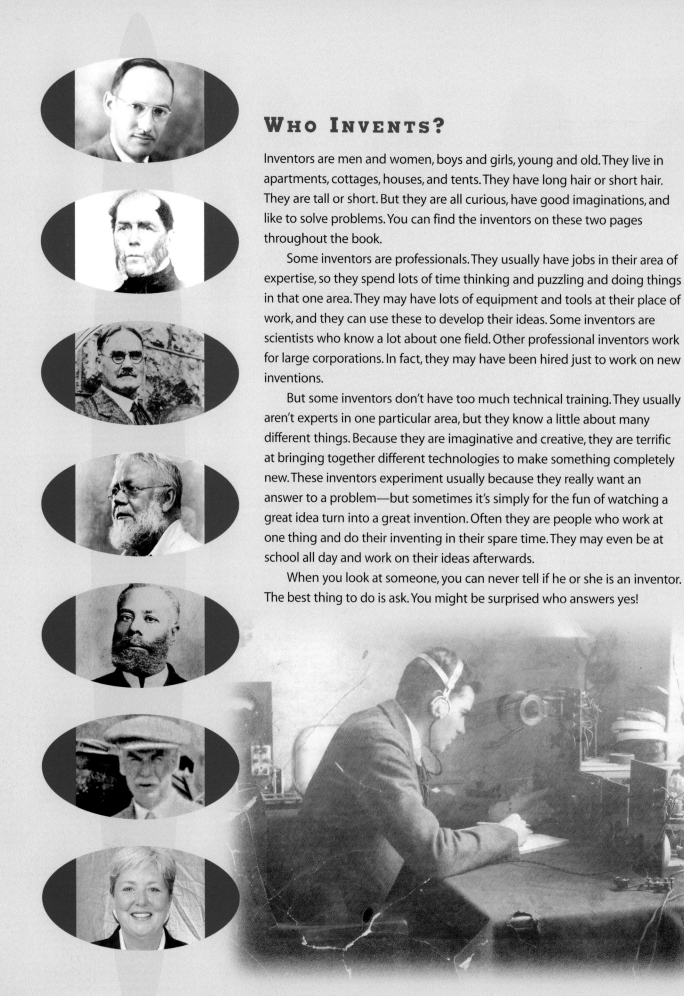

WHO INVENTS?

Inventors are men and women, boys and girls, young and old. They live in apartments, cottages, houses, and tents. They have long hair or short hair. They are tall or short. But they are all curious, have good imaginations, and like to solve problems. You can find the inventors on these two pages throughout the book.

Some inventors are professionals. They usually have jobs in their area of expertise, so they spend lots of time thinking and puzzling and doing things in that one area. They may have lots of equipment and tools at their place of work, and they can use these to develop their ideas. Some inventors are scientists who know a lot about one field. Other professional inventors work for large corporations. In fact, they may have been hired just to work on new inventions.

But some inventors don't have too much technical training. They usually aren't experts in one particular area, but they know a little about many different things. Because they are imaginative and creative, they are terrific at bringing together different technologies to make something completely new. These inventors experiment usually because they really want an answer to a problem—but sometimes it's simply for the fun of watching a great idea turn into a great invention. Often they are people who work at one thing and do their inventing in their spare time. They may even be at school all day and work on their ideas afterwards.

When you look at someone, you can never tell if he or she is an inventor. The best thing to do is ask. You might be surprised who answers yes!

CANADA INVENTS

Inventors live in all countries of the world. This book is called *Canada Invents*, and the inventions included were made by people who either came to live in Canada, were born here, or once lived here. You'll notice that some of the inventions in this book were made by the ancestors of the Inuit, perhaps even before they came to the land now known as Canada. This seems like just the right place to recognize them. This book also includes Alexander Graham Bell, who was born in Scotland and then lived in Canada and the United States. So you see—a Canadian invention can be a very flexible thing!

YOUNG MINDS

You are never too young to have a great idea, and these Canadians prove it! Gina Gallant was eleven when she made her first invention, a cracker that doesn't get soggy when it's put in soup. Alexander Graham Bell was fourteen when he invented a rotary brush device to remove husks from wheat. Joseph-Armand Bombardier began developing the first snowmobile when he was fifteen.

7

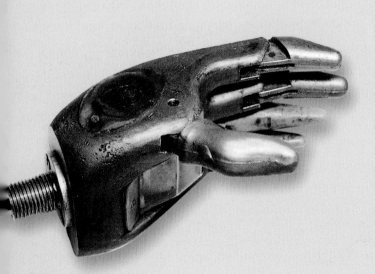

WHAT'S AHEAD

Although it would be great to include every Canadian invention, that would need a much longer book— maybe a whole series of books! What you will find as you read on is a sampling of some famous and not-so-famous inventions, some inventions from long ago, and some current inventions. They are all fascinating, and so are the people who created them. Who knows? Maybe after you've been introduced to them, a light bulb will go off in your mind. You may even be inspired to do a little inventing yourself!

Snow and Ice

Inventions to Cope with Canada's Cold

Brrrrr, brrrr, brrrr … Yes, it's true. For many months of the year, Canadians spend a lot of time shivering. That's natural in a place that is covered in snow and ice and reaches very low temperatures during the winter. But the white stuff hasn't stopped Canadians from rising to the challenges that their climate presents. In fact, ever since people first came to this country, they have been finding solutions to the problems that snow and ice bring.

When you have a problem and add a little ingenuity, the result is often an invention. So what do you get when you combine lots of snow and ice with lots of creativity (and some chattering teeth)? Lots of Canadian inventions. Slip on a parka, wrap a scarf around your neck, and read on!

Sled and Tread and Eat

The ancestors of the Inuit were inventors extraordinaire. They had to be. Scientists say they arrived in Canada's north by crossing the Bering Strait, and were confronted with snow and ice—lots of it!

These early Arctic dwellers had to travel across the snow carrying burdens such as meat. They could carry only so much on their backs, so how were they to cope? One solution was to fill a polar bear hide with items and drag it along. But someone must have got fed up with the hard work of hauling and decided to create something that could slide. Final product? The *komatik*. This long sled was made up of ladder-like crossbars of bone or wood joining two runners, with handlebars made of caribou antlers or bone. When hunters piled their game on it and pulled, it moved fairly easily across the snowy ground.

Over time the sled's runners often got damaged by rocks or rough ice. No problem. Those creative minds had another idea. Ivory plates, or "sled shoes," were attached to protect the runners from wear and tear. At the same time, the people pulling the *komatik* invented ice-creepers to prevent *themselves* from slipping on the ice. Strips of bone or ivory with "treads," or sharp notches, cut into them, ice-creepers provided instant traction when attached to the bottoms of boots. Of course, eventually using husky dogs to pull the sleds was an even better solution.

Harpoons were invented to spear whales and seals, but they were useless for catching ducks and geese. Eventually, hunger probably led to the invention of the *bola*. This "flying" weapon was made of bone weights joined together by strings. When a hunter threw the *bola*, the weights pulled apart and the weapon whirled through the air like a pinwheel. The unsuspecting bird would become tangled in the strings and fall to the ground. Dinner, anyone?

■ An Inuit man works on the runners of his overturned sled, or *komatik*. Eventually, people learned to let dog teams do the hard work of pulling the sleds (above).

SNOW GOGGLES

■ This Inuit man is wearing snow goggles made from driftwood. The narrow openings protect his eyes from snow-blindness by letting only a small amount of sunlight through.

Have you ever noticed that you have to squint when you are out in the snow on a sunny day? That's because the ultraviolet light of the sun isn't easily absorbed by the white snow. It bounces off—straight into your eyes. When you spend lots of time outside on snowy, sunny days, your corneas can become damaged by the light if you aren't wearing sunglasses or goggles to protect your eyes.

This is not news to the Inuit who live in northern Canada, where there is snow for many months of the year. In fact, it was likely their ancestors who invented the first snow goggles thousands of years ago. They knew first-hand that without eye protection, they could become snow-blind. Their solution? They experimented with carving slits in whale bone, ivory, or even wood. They then wore these "snow goggles" like glasses (see left). The chance of snow-blindness was reduced. Mission accomplished.

DISTANT COUSINS?

Was the toboggan a descendant of the *komatik*? Perhaps. And what about the concrete toboggan? What? You've never heard of this bizarre invention?

Every year since the mid-1970s, undergraduate engineering students from Canada, the United States, and abroad have been participating in the Great Northern Concrete Toboggan Race. Teams design their own toboggans according to certain rules: they must have room for five riders; they must have a total mass of less than 136 kilograms; and they must have a concrete running surface. The toboggans must also have a fixed roll bar for safety purposes, and all riders must wear helmets. These crazy vehicles are then raced down a 150-metre racing course.

Points are awarded for times, design, and general presentation (which includes team spirit). And because the braking system is extremely important, teams lose points for each rider ejected from the toboggan during braking.

How fast do they go? Well, in 1998 *Thunder* was officially declared the fastest concrete toboggan in the world, clocking in at a speed of fifty kilometres (31 miles) an hour. That's one flying piece of concrete!

Building an igloo (at left and above), using snow knives to cut the blocks of snow.

Igloo Plus

Imagine it's bedtime. You start to yawn, but where do you head for a warm, comfortable sleep when all around you is only snow and ice? The Inuit ancestors learned to make do with what they had. They used the wind-packed snow of the tundra to create a shelter. *Igloo* is the Inuit word for "house."

But what tool could they use to cut the wind-packed snow into blocks? Enter another technological invention, the snow knife. It was large and flat and made of whale bone or ivory. With it, blocks of snow were carved out of the ground from an area that would become the house floor and entranceway. (One section was left untouched to be used as an interior platform.) The snow blocks were placed side by side and shaped into a sturdy dome-like structure. The design had to be just right so the snow house didn't collapse in a disappointing heap. It would be fascinating to know how many failures came before the ultimate success—a safe and windproof igloo.

An Inuit woman tends a seal-oil lamp inside an igloo in the western Arctic.

SOAPSTONE LAMP

When an igloo was complete, there was a platform along the back that was higher than the floor. Warm air rises and would collect here, making this one of the warmest places in the snow house! Babies were put here to play, and the family slept together here. This was also a good place for a soapstone lamp.

The Inuit ancestors had discovered a way to get oil from the fat (or blubber) of the sea mammals they hunted. When they learned that they could burn this oil, the invention of the blubber lamp was not far behind. The lamp that held the oil was usually made out of pottery or soapstone, and the wick was made from moss. When the oil burned, it gave off both light and heat—without smoke. Perfect for a snow house.

WALKING ON SNOW

Native Canadians of the subarctic who had to cope with snowy winters certainly made and used snowshoes. Different tribes even came up with their own designs. Snowshoes ranged in shape (from round to oval to pointy), in length (from one to almost two metres), and surface (some were flat and some turned up at the toe). With snowshoes strapped on, a person would have his weight spread out so he could move across the snow—instead of sinking into it.

But were snowshoes actually invented by Native Canadians? Archaeologists think not. They believe snowshoes were invented in Asia about six thousand years ago. How did they get to North America? On the feet of the first travellers to cross the Bering Strait. Perhaps these adventurers never would have made the trip successfully if the snowshoe hadn't been invented.

■ This photo shows the Jull Centrifugal Snow Excavator. Above, a rotary snowplow is at work clearing snow along the rail lines on the White Pass and Yukon route.

ROTARY SNOWPLOW

In the nineteenth century, the dawning age of machines, there was going to be even more trouble with snow. How, for example, could a railway track be kept clear so that a train, a crucial part of early Canada's transportation system, could travel along it unimpeded? Trains already had cowcatchers on the front of their engines to "catch," or push, unwary cows off the tracks, but they didn't do the trick when a train had to move through snow mounds or even mountain avalanches. The wedge snowplow, which was like a larger

cowcatcher on the front of the engine, was an improvement, but if it hit packed snow, the inadequate plow would jump the track, leaving the snow on the rails.

It took a Toronto dentist to come up with the best solution! In 1869, J. W. Elliott invented the rotary snowplow. This machine, which attached to the front of the engine, was like a revolving snow shovel. Snow was scooped off the tracks and moved to revolving fan-like steel plates, which threw the snow out of the way of the train.

The invention worked quite well, but the railways weren't very interested in it—until a man named Orange Jull added a cutting wheel to the front of the blower. When it was tested in 1880, the successful blower threw ice to a distance of sixty metres! A few more changes were made—an ice cutter was added, along with a larger scoop wheel for lifting snow—and soon the rotary snowplow was being used on railways throughout Canada and the United States.

SNOW BLOWER

Okay, so there were snowplows for trains, but what about roads and highways? Arthur Sicard of Montreal, Quebec, got on the job. After years of work, he invented a self-propelled snow blower that allowed a single operator to clear snow, whether it was hard, soft, or packed, and throw it more than thirty metres, either to the side of the road or into a dump truck. In 1927, he made his first sale. Soon snow blowers were seen on the roads of Quebec and then throughout Canada. Sicard's invention even made it onto a commemorative Canadian fifty-cent stamp, and there is now a street in Bécancour, Quebec, named after him!

■ Arthur Sicard sold his first snow blower to the municipality of Outremont, in Montreal, in 1927.

HEATED ROADS

When Jim Beaudoin and his team came along, suddenly there was talk of getting rid of snow and ice on roads by *melting* it away. Doctors Beaudoin, Ping Xie, Ping Gu, and Yan Fu, researchers at Canada's National Research Council, began brainstorming about concrete in 1972. They saw that concrete on some major highways was corroding because of the huge amounts of salt put on the roads to melt ice and snow during Canada's long, severe winters. They wondered if they could change the concrete so that snow wouldn't stay on it and salt wouldn't be needed, allowing the concrete to last a lot longer.

What did they do? They replaced the sand and gravel in normal concrete with small particles of a carbon material called coke-breeze (a cheap and available waste product of steel-making processes). They called their new material conductive concrete, and it proved to be just as strong as regular concrete. It had an amazing difference, though: the materials that made up their concrete could conduct electricity. You can plug in the concrete, switch it on, and it will warm up. The heat spreads, and any snow on top melts away! If you sandwich it between two layers of normal concrete, it is shockproof. In 1995, the inventors received a patent for their incredible concrete. It is only a matter of time before it will be used to de-ice roads, sidewalks, and bridges, or even to warm a parking pad for aircraft.

■ Dr. Jim Beaudoin stands on a "plugged-in" concrete slab that will stay snow- and ice-free all winter.

Joseph-Armand Bombardier

When Joseph-Armand Bombardier was a young boy, he loved building things. He collected unwanted materials and used them to build mechanical toys. He taught himself how motors and engines worked by fiddling with them, and he soon learned how to repair broken engines.

Curious and imaginative, Bombardier began experimenting, trying to create new things with old parts. When he was fifteen, he built a steam engine powered with the air from an inflated car tire. That same year, Bombardier pursued one of his dreams: to come up with an efficient way to travel over snow. He put a car engine (from an old Model T Ford) on a four-runnered wooden sleigh, and then hooked a propeller to the back of the engine. On January 31, 1922, Bombardier and his brother, Léopold, hopped on to their invention, turned on the unmuffled motor, and to the alarm of pedestrians, test-drove the first motorized snow vehicle down the streets of Valcourt, Quebec, pulling on ropes to steer (more or less) its front runners.

Four years later, in May 1926, Bombardier opened Garage Bombardier. Although he was already known in his own town for his inventions, he soon became known far and wide for his great mechanical skill and his ability to solve problems. Couldn't find the equipment he needed? He'd make it himself. No electricity in his garage? He'd build his own hydroelectric plant by damming the river.

Winters were slow at the garage, however. There was no snow-clearing machinery yet, so snow kept all the local cars at home. This gave Bombardier time to think—and a problem to solve. What kind of vehicle would allow people to get around easily in the winter snow? His solution? The auto-neige (snow car). He moved the front wheels of a normal car closer together so they could fit in the grooves left in

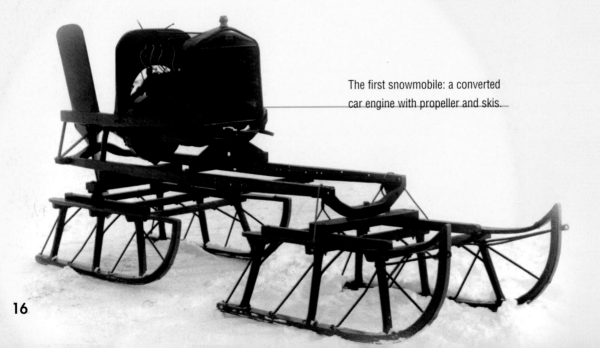

The first snowmobile: a converted car engine with propeller and skis.

the snow by horse-drawn carriages. He then added an extra set of wheels on the back and put chains around them for added traction. In 1931, he replaced the four back wheels with six smaller wheels and a rubber track.

And yet, his snow vehicles were still not perfect. After his son died during the winter of 1935 because Bombardier could not get him through the blocked roads to the closest hospital, he became even more determined to invent a reliable snow vehicle. The very next year, he successfully designed a seven-passenger snow vehicle, the B7 (B for Bombardier and 7 because it could carry seven passengers). It wasn't long before he'd invented the larger B12.

Bombardier didn't stop there. He was full of great ideas and passionate about vehicles. He invented the BT, which, with its winch and loading platform, replaced the horse-drawn sleigh that loggers used. In the 1950s, he invented the TN (a truck-like snowmobile that could travel over muskeg), the Muskeg Tractor, and the Muskeg Carrier.

Also during the 1950s, Bombardier began working on a one-person *auto-neige* that people would be able to drive anywhere there was snow. The final product was to be called the Ski-Dog, because Bombardier thought it might replace the dogsled in the North. If you think you haven't heard of one, think again. When the Ski-Dog logo was printed, the *g* in

"dog" was either incorrectly printed as an *o* or so small that it looked like an *o*. Everyone mistakenly thought the new machine was called a Ski-Doo, and the name stuck. The design was patented in 1959, and the Ski-Doo was soon as popular then as it is today.

The first Ski-Doo, 1959.

Ski-Doo 2002, Olympic Edition.

Bombardier's company still exists, and he would probably have been pleased that it didn't just stick with the machines he himself had created. Today, Bombardier Incorporated is a world leader that designs and manufactures Sea-Doos (which is like a Ski-Doo for water), subway cars, airplanes, and even aerospace equipment.

17

ICY WINGS

Even off the roads, the trouble with ice doesn't stop. Thick layers often form on the wings and propellers of airplanes travelling through cold weather. The dangers are obvious: the weight of the ice can cause the airplane to crash.

In the 1930s, a "rubber overshoe" was invented to cope with ice on airplane wings. Placed on the front edge of a wing, the rubber overshoe would be inflated to break away any ice that accumulated. But ice also was a problem on propellers. There was a method that used an anti-freeze solution in the hub of the propeller, but this did not always work.

Then John Orr and T. R. Griffith, researchers at the National Research Council, turned their creative minds to the problem. After years of research, they put the finishing touches on a new type of de-icer in 1943. Specially manufactured rubber strips with wires running through them were attached to the edges of airplane propellers. The heater wires were connected to a generator attached to the hub of the propeller. Electricity ran along the wires, heating up the layer of conducting rubber, and the heat either prevented ice from forming or melted ice that was already there. Many lives were saved by this valuable Canadian invention.

■ Scenes like this are a thing of the past—thanks to Orr and Griffith's propeller de-icer.

Up to Your Knees in Snow

During winter in Canada, the depth of snow is measured once a day at many climatological stations. Why? Knowing the depth of snow on the ground can be important. Farmers, foresters, flood control forecasters, highway maintenance crews, and ski resort operators all need this vital information.

Bob Wilson was an old hand at taking snow measurements. He had spent many years as a weather observer, four of them in the Arctic. One day, while he was working as a technologist at Environment Canada, Wilson teamed up with two colleagues, John Metcalfe and Barry Goodison, to work on a new idea. The three men wanted to invent a way of measuring snow depth without having to trudge out with a snow ruler and calculate it by hand. "There were a large number of unmanned remote weather stations which could use instruments to gather basic meteorological data," recalls Wilson, "but there was no instrument to take any snow-depth measurements!" An automatic snow-depth sensor was needed.

By about 1980, Wilson, Metcalfe, and Goodison were developing the prototype of their device, and by 1986, the final product had been licensed for distribution. Here's how it works. A sensor, mounted at a fixed height from the ground, sends out an ultrasonic pulse. The pulse travels down to the snow and then bounces back from the surface up to the sensor. The time the pulse takes to make its journey is measured. The shorter the time, the deeper the snow!

Now snow depth can be measured at northern weather stations without anyone even being there. And that's not all. "Air-traffic control systems at American airports often use a similar device to adjust the calibration of their landing systems when the snow depth exceeds two feet," says Wilson. "And some countries use the device to determine the depth of sand in desert fringe areas to measure the movement of desert boundaries."

■ Thanks to the snow-depth sensor, data can be gathered even at extremely remote—and unstaffed—weather stations.

SNOW DOME

Randy Buhler has always been interested in snow structures, and every winter he would make one: a snow cave, a tunnel, a quinzhee, and yes, even an igloo. And yet, says Buhler, "I was always frustrated at the length of time it took to make these structures. I was also unimpressed with the irregular shapes, low ceilings, and small living area that were the results of my efforts." The solution? Invent a new snow structure that has plenty of space and doesn't take a long time to build.

Buhler stayed up late one night, sketching. He wanted to create the perfect dome. He thought about his old ideas, but there were problems with all of them. Suddenly, he got a brainwave. The answer wasn't to create something *onto* which snow could be piled, but to create something *into* which snow could be shovelled. He came up with the idea of collapsible fabric panels that can be used to make a mould. The panels can be laced together and filled with snow. The snow is then packed into the form of an igloo and the panels are peeled off. Now Randy sells these panels in kits to Boy Scout and Girl Guide groups, winter campers, and any other people raring for a hands-on snowy adventure.

■ Randy Buhler's pre-fabricated Polar Dome is a new kind of igloo that is made without blocks.

A QUIN ... WHAT?

A quinzhee. Now that's a word to look up in the dictionary. And here's what it will tell you: "A shelter created by piling up snow, letting it settle, and then hollowing out the interior."

Ka-boom!

Inventions of Energy and Power

Probably from the day the first human realized that it was warmer to stand in the sun than in the shade, people have been alert to energy sources. After all, we need energy to stay alive! We use energy to light our lives. We use it to grow food and to cook our food. We use it to stay warm and to stay cool. We have learned to use it to power machines, such as cars, trains, computers, and Ferris wheels.

Where does energy come from? Creative minds through the centuries have figured out how to use energy from the sun, from water and wind, and from fire. Inventors have also discovered how to create energy with steam, how to release energy locked in minerals, and even how to split atoms to create nuclear energy.

The next few pages will introduce you to some important Canadian contributions to both making and saving energy.

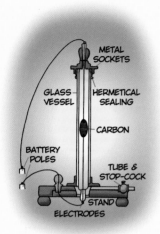

Everyone knows that Thomas Edison invented the light bulb. Right? Wrong. Meet Henry Woodward, a medical student from Toronto, Ontario. Back in 1873, a few years before anyone had ever heard of Thomas Edison, Woodward and a friend, Matthew Evans, a Toronto hotel-keeper, invented the first light bulb. It was a glass bulb containing a carbon filament and nitrogen gas. The bulb was sealed to keep in the nitrogen.

Woodward and Evans tested their filament bulb until they were sure it worked properly, then they patented it in Toronto in 1875. But unfortunately, the two inventors couldn't raise enough money to develop, produce, and sell the light bulbs. So only one year later, the patent was sold to an American fellow who had been working on a similar invention. His name was Thomas Edison.

Some say that the light bulb Edison "invented" was an improvement on the Woodward and Evans bulb. Others say that it was practically identical to it. Still others say that Woodward's bulb was more advanced because it used nitrogen, as our bulbs do today. In any case, whenever you flip that switch and the light bulb turns on, you owe it to two Canadians.

HOW DO THEY WORK?

Electricity is created by the flow of electrons. A filament is a thin material that resists the flow of electrons through it. When the flow of electrons is slowed down, this causes friction, and friction causes heat. When a filament in a bulb heats up, it glows, or becomes incandescent. To prevent the filament from burning, the oxygen inside the light bulb is sucked out and the bulb is sealed. Woodward used a carbon filament, which burned quite easily. Today a material called tungsten is used for filaments. Tungsten is one of the hardest known metals and can heat up to high temperatures without melting.

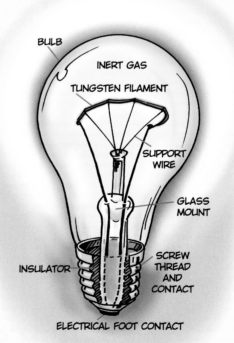

CARBIDE WILLSON

Enough is enough! After performing one too many smelly experiments in the laboratory he had built in his family's basement, young Thomas Willson began to search for another place to conduct his tests. He was given a room above the local blacksmith's shop in exchange for his help around the forge.

But it turned out that the blacksmith was just as eager to help Thomas with his experiments. Together, the two invented a system of experimental arc lights. It was 1881, and there had never been an electric light in Hamilton, Ontario. It must have been startling to walk past the smithy at night and see the newfangled glow from the second-floor lab.

Willson got a patent for the arc lights before he was even twenty-one.

But he didn't stop there. He had a great imagination, worked hard, and had some good luck. He began experimenting with combining and heating different types of materials. When he heated a combination of coal, lime, and tar to very high temperatures, he accidentally created a greyish mixture—calcium carbide. By mixing calcium carbide with water, he produced a gas—acetylene gas. Calcium carbide and acetylene weren't new, but Thomas had discovered the inexpensive process for making them. And he also figured out that acetylene could best be used for the bright light it makes when it burns.

Willson and his partners patented the carbide process, then sold the patent to an American company, the Union Carbide Company. Willson kept the Canadian rights and began setting up factories in Ontario and Quebec. Carbide plants need lots of power for their furnaces, so at his first factory, in Merritton, Ontario (near St. Catharines), he also built the first Canadian hydroelectric plant.

Acetylene was used in street lights and navigational buoys, and it is still used today in materials from plastics to synthetic rubber. But perhaps its most important use was as the heat source in the oxy-acetylene torch, which was invented in 1903. This torch could weld and also cut thick plates of steel into any shape. Think of how this amazing technology has affected the automobile and shipbuilding industries. Without the oxy-acetylene torch and Thomas "Carbide" Willson's process that made the production of acetylene possible, the world of transportation would be very different today.

■ *Above:* Thomas "Carbide" Willson at age fifty-four. *Right:* Canada's first calcium carbide plant, in Merritton, Ontario.

YEAST WITH ENERGY

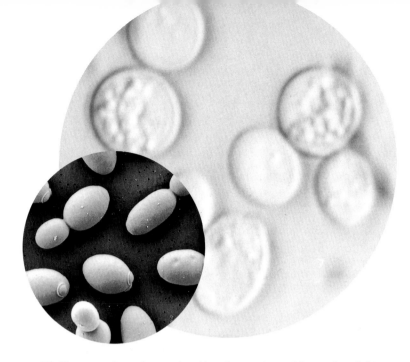

These two photomicrographs of brewing yeast were taken under a light microscope and an electron microscope.

Imagine inventing a super yeast that can produce alcohol—and then discovering that the same yeast can also power a car. Well, that's what happened to Inge Russell when she was working in the research department at a large Canadian brewery, Labatt, in the 1980s. Breweries make beer, and beer is made with yeast, which is a living micro-organism. The goal of the Labatt team was to develop a new strain of yeast that would produce a beer that fermented faster and had a better flavour. Using a special process, Russell joined together strains of yeast that would not have joined naturally. One of the strains she invented seemed to be just right. There was only one problem: "If I used it for beer," Russell remembers, "the taste was terrible!"

But she realized that her super yeast could be used for something else. "For fuel alcohol, it was superb," she says. And what is fuel alcohol? "It is used for fuel for cars, instead of gasoline," Russell explains. "Many countries that have a large supply of fermentable carbohydrates, such as sugar cane, will ferment it and use it for fuel instead of importing expensive gasoline."

Labatt patented the super yeast and then sold the strain to the Lallemand Yeast Company, one of the largest yeast producers in the world. Now Lallemand is successfully selling Russell's strain of yeast to the fuel-alcohol industry worldwide.

PARK AND FRY

Is it possible to power a tractor with grease from french fries? After eight years of research, David Boocock, of the University of Toronto, found a way to change cooking oils into diesel fuel, which he has named Biodiesel. Since 1999, the smelliest grease from restaurants, food-processing companies, or anywhere else food is fried has been able to run a school bus. Plus, the fuel burns cleanly—and smells like french fries!

■ Unlike most vehicles, this bus in downtown Vancouver doesn't cause pollution. It emits only water and heat.

GO WITHOUT GAS

Fuel cells are devices that convert the chemical energy of a fuel into electricity to generate power. Instead of using up non-renewable resources, like oil, they use oxygen from the air and hydrogen (or a mixture containing hydrogen). Hydrogen is the most abundant element on earth. And fuel cells emit only water and heat.

Fuel cells aren't new—they were first invented in 1839—but they had no practical application until recently. In the 1960s, they provided electricity for the Gemini and Apollo spacecraft, and by the 1980s, they were being tested by electricity providers and car manufacturers.

Fuel cells are now being made by many companies around the world, but the leader in the development of one type, the proton exchange membrane (PEM) fuel cell, is Ballard Power Systems Inc. This Vancouver-based company was formed in 1979 by Geoff Ballard. It develops and manufactures the Ballard Fuel Cell, which is the world's most advanced, publicly demonstrated PEM fuel cell. The company has applied for more than 355 patents worldwide covering inventions relating to PEM fuel-cell technology.

In 1998, Ballard began a public demonstration of its prototype zero-emission engine in transit buses. In January 2000, the company unveiled the Mark 900, a smaller and more advanced PEM fuel cell for transportation applications. Ballard fuel cells are now powering many prototype products, including automobiles and buses. Some of them are in use on the streets of Chicago and Vancouver, so if you get a chance, hop on for a clean ride.

Abraham Gesner

Young Abraham Gesner had a passion for rocks and minerals—and this would lead to one of the most important inventions in Canadian history.

Gesner was born in 1797, on a farm in the Cornwallis valley on the west side of what would one day be Nova Scotia. When he was born, Canada was not even a country yet—and wouldn't be for another seventy years. There were roads for horses, but they were too rough for wagons. And it would be almost a century before the car was invented!

Gesner grew up loving the countryside and wandering the fields and beaches with his best friend, Bill Webster. As the tide went out in the Bay of Fundy, the semi-precious stones and fossils of the cliffs were exposed. The boys would collect specimens and haul them back home.

Because they wanted to support their son's interests, Gesner's parents encouraged his studies and converted an old shed on their property into a laboratory for their son. It was here that Gesner did his early experimenting, trying to find ways to unlock the heat and light contained within rocks and minerals. One early success came when he learned to make matches by coating one end of a thin sliver of wood with a paste of potassium chlorate and sulphur. Matches were not at all common in the early 1800s, and Gesner began to carry them with him wherever he went.

When Gesner was a young man, he helped out on the family farm for a while. But times became tough in the local communities. So adventurous Abraham, determined to help make ends meet, began taking horses by sailing ship to sell in the West Indies. On one cold December trip, he and his mates were shipwrecked. Cold and wet, they might have died if Gesner had not pulled out two waterproof metal boxes. He took a match out of one and dipped it into the other container, which contained oil of vitriol. When he lifted up

In 1842, Gesner opened a small museum to display his own collections of fossils, shells, and minerals— the first museum in Canada.

This main street was brightened at night by one of Gesner's kerosene lamps.

the match, exposing it to the air, it burst into flame. A roaring fire was soon drying off the amazed and grateful crew.

Gesner's business dealings were not very successful, but happily, Harriet Webster, his friend Bill's sister, agreed to marry him anyway. Since he was in debt up to his eyeballs—and indeed was facing prison—Abraham couldn't refuse when Harriet's father insisted on paying for him to travel to London, England, to study medicine. Although he really wanted to study geology, Gesner reluctantly went overseas. When he returned home in 1827, he quickly set up practice in Parrsboro, Nova Scotia, but he spent all his spare time studying and mapping the geology of Nova Scotia, and writing back and forth to other geologists around the world about his discoveries and ideas. In 1838, he was appointed New Brunswick's official geologist, and it must have seemed like his greatest dreams had finally come true. He surveyed the vast area by horseback, making geological maps and speculating, perhaps too enthusiastically, about possible mining opportunities.

Gesner was dismissed five years later, and he returned to Nova Scotia to practice again as a medical doctor—but he was determined to continue to dream, experiment, and invent. Intrigued by the new science of current electricity, he built a small motor that converted mechanical energy into direct electric current and a machine that insulated electrical wire. But electricity was still a novelty at the time. The light bulb hadn't been invented yet—and even the bicycle had been invented only five years earlier.

Although he was intrigued by electricity,

Gesner never abandoned his passion for rocks and minerals. He invented coal briquettes that burned evenly, a useful invention at a time when coal was used to warm homes. He then began to focus on making a better lighting fuel. In the 1840s, the only light in homes came from tallow candles, expensive whale- or seal-oil lamps, or the volatile camphene. In 1846, Gesner discovered that if he burned coal, or coal-like substances like asphaltum or the albertite, it gave off a gas. When he condensed this gas, it turned into a liquid. If he let it sit, the liquid separated into oil and water. To his delight, he discovered that the oil could be burned to produce a light.

But the light wasn't very bright, so Gesner continued his experiments until he had uncovered the best process for making the oil. Gesner called this oil, which he perfected in 1853, kerosene (from the Greek kero, meaning "wax," and sene, meaning "oil"). It produced a better and safer light than any of the other oils being used at the time.

Imagine how kerosene changed people's daily lives. When it got dark at night, it was cheap and safe to simply light a kerosene lamp. Instead of going to bed, people could work longer, read, sew, or play games—all by the light of the incredible kerosene lamp. Although electric light bulbs were invented in the 1870s, power lines did not reach many urban homes until the early 1900s—and in the country, even later. As a result, kerosene continued to be used widely for decades.

Kerosene let families have more time together.

Kerosene was an important invention, but so was Gesner's refining process. After he showed that many useful materials could come from refined coal, others decided to try to refine crude oil or petroleum. They discovered that these would form different liquids that could be separated into various types of oils, chemicals, and gasoline and then used in many ways. Today, diesel fuel, plastics, fertilizers, detergents, paints, textiles, and gasoline are all made from petroleum products.

Some inventors apply for a patent to protect their inventions. A patent gives a person or an organization—and nobody else—the right to make, use, or sell an invention. There have been more than one million patents registered in Canada, with the one-millionth granted in 1976. A Canadian, James Guillet, and Dr. Harvey Troth, a British researcher, had invented a new plastic that turned to dust if it was constantly exposed to sunlight.

WHAT A GAS!

In 1994, two creative teenagers from London, Ontario, were concerned about the environment and tried to think of ways to degrade waste products. Almost by accident, Ram Puvanesasingham and Chris Heyn invented an award-winning plastic gas. Using the lab at Heyn's high school, they heated plastic. When it melted, it produced a gas. The teens had set up a distillation apparatus so they could collect the gas and distil it. The end result was a liquid. When they analyzed it, they realized that among other things, it contained ethanol and so could be a useful fuel additive.

When ethanol is added to gasoline, the gasoline combusts better and burns more efficiently. "You end up producing less pollutants when you burn gasoline with a certain percentage of ethanol," explains Puvanesasingham. This dynamic young duo won a Manning Young Canadian Innovation Award for their exciting invention.

■ Chris Heyn (left) and Ram Puvanesasingham (right) receive the Manning Young Canadian Innovation Award from Dr. Tom Calvert of the Manning Foundation.

Saving Energy

What would you name this invention? A sensor, about the size of a computer mouse, is connected by a flexible cord to an electronic circuit box, which can connect to any computer. When it's placed up against materials, the sensor gets hot, then transfers the heat to the material. It then measures the material's thermal conductivity—its ability to absorb that heat.

Nancy Mathis, originally of PEI and now based in Fredericton, New Brunswick, decided to call her invention the TC (for "thermal conductivity") Probe. Before the TC Probe came along in 1997, the only way to check the thermal conductivity of any given material was to actually set it on fire.

But why do we need to check the ability of a material to absorb heat? Well, for one thing, a material that absorbs lots of heat tends to be very flammable, which means it can heat up too much and burst into flames. So the TC Probe is often used to test any materials that are exposed to heat. Mathis hopes it will help prevent fires in aircraft, homes, cars, and computers. "What we're doing with the probe will give you warmer houses, more useable space inside your refrigerator, computers that last longer, and alternative materials so car manufacturers can make lighter cars and save energy," she says.

■ Nancy Mathis hopes the TC Probe will lead to a more energy-efficient world.

Sun Energy

In the mid-1990s, John Hollick of Perth, Ontario, developed Solarwall, an award-winning solar heating system for houses, office buildings, and warehouses. Now Canada has the tallest solar collector and the largest solar air-heating system in the world!

■ This Solarwall at Bombardier is the world's largest solar air-heating system.

GREEN MACHINE

Paul Brown and Anie Galipeau believe their Green Walkman will virtually eliminate the environmental damage caused by discarded batteries.

Nineteen-year-old Paul Brown was busing into high school one morning in December 1992 when the batteries on his portable cassette player, or Walkman, began to die. He stuck a pencil in the machine sprockets and began to turn it steadily, helping along the fading batteries. Surprisingly, he was able to continue to listen to his music all the rest of the way to school. That's when it hit him. He and a classmate, Anie Galipeau, had been looking for a project to complete for their design and technology class—and this was it.

"In 1992, there were over a billion batteries being thrown out every year, and now there are probably even more," says Galipeau. "Discarded batteries leach huge amounts of toxic chemicals into the groundwater." Their project, the Green Walkman, sought to replace the batteries used in tape cassettes and help out the environment.

By June 1993, the prototype was complete. Instead of being powered by batteries, the Green Walkman uses a spring mechanism wound by a clock key. "We built it with recycled clock parts," remembers Galipeau. "And we didn't have any precision tools, only a drill press. Our Green Walkman prototype … plays at a constant speed for thirty to forty-five minutes before it needs to be rewound."

In 1999, Brown and Galipeau received a U.S. patent for their technology, and they are now going to try to apply it to CD players—and maybe even cellphones and pagers.

Fun and Games

Canada is a country full of people who like to have fun. Canadians have adapted or changed games from other countries to suit their own special needs, and they have come up with their own completely original ideas about how to enjoy themselves. Read on to find out about just some of the stick-whacking, ball-slamming, disc-shooting, puzzle-piecing, question-stumping inventions that were grown in Canada.

"He Shoots! He Scores!"

Because Canadian winters are so long and cold, it makes sense to have a game that *has* to be played on ice. When the temperatures drop to well below freezing, children and adults all across the country head out to frozen ponds, lakes, and ice rinks to chase a puck with a stick and try to put it into a net. Hockey, a combination of European and Native ball-and-stick games, is a Canadian invention. But it is a competitive sport, and perhaps this explains why no one can agree on where the first hockey game was played or by whom. (Nova Scotia or Ontario? The early settlers or soldiers?) No one can even agree on the location of the first *organized* hockey game. (Was it Halifax, Montreal, or Toronto? Take your pick!)

What does seem certain is that the first indoor hockey game was played on March 3, 1875, in Montreal at the Victoria Skating Rink. After this game, hockey became even more popular, and leagues began to form in different cities. In 1886, the Amateur Hockey Association released the first set of formal rules for the popular game. In 1917, the professional National Hockey League (NHL) was formed in Montreal.

■ By 1900, hockey had extended its reach to the farthest corners of Canada, as this game in Dawson, Yukon, shows.

FIRST HOCKEY STICKS

A group of Native Canadians, the Mi'kmaq, had long been carving curved sticks to use when they played Oochamkunutk, an ice game similar to hockey. When hockey became popular, they began to carve and sell hockey sticks. Soon the popularity of hockey outstripped their ability to supply sticks. When the Starr Manufacturing Company, of Dartmouth, Nova Scotia, began making a hockey stick from yellow birch, it named the stick the MicMac, in honour of these early Native carvers.

Skates

The first skates were probably invented in Scandinavia more than two thousand years ago. But since then, there have been many Canadian improvements made. James Whelpley, of New Brunswick, invented the Long Reach skate in 1857, when he was about eighteen years old. He began manufacturing them two years later. The blade of the Long Reach was forty-three centimetres long and extended beyond the front and back of the skater's boot.

At this time, skates had to be fastened to a skater's boots with leather straps and buckles. In 1865, however, John Forbes of the Starr Manufacturing Company, invented the world's first self-fastening skate. This had a blade that could be clamped into place under the skater's boot in less than a minute. It was sturdy and safe, and it didn't fall off when skaters made quick turns!

By 1900, skaters weren't wearing any old pair of boots when they went skating. Special skating boots had been invented to give extra support to the skater's ankles. Soon Starr Manufacturing invented the tube skate, which screwed onto the bottom of a skater's skating boots. The tubes were lighter and tougher than the single-blade skates, and they wouldn't crack or break as easily if they were hit by a puck.

■ Early goalie masks, like Clint Benedict's (top) and Jacques Plante's (bottom), had an almost primitive feel.

■ Thanks in large part to companies like Starr Manufacturing, skating became a sport everyone could enjoy. This Ottawa skating party in the late 1800s includes (at left) Princess Louise, the daughter of Queen Victoria, and Canada's governor general, the Marquis of Lorne.

Goalie Mask

The first goalie ever to wear a mask was Clint Benedict, of the Montreal Maroons, in the late 1920s. But he found it too difficult to play hockey while sporting the leather-and-wire mask, so he wore it only once. In the 1960s, Jacques Plante, an all-star goalie with the Montreal Canadiens, invented a much more practical mask. By 1959, he had been hit repeatedly in the face with flying pucks. A broken nose, broken cheekbones, and a broken jaw—it was too much. So Plante, working with Fiberglas Canada, developed a moulded fibreglass hockey mask that covered his entire face. Pucks still hurt when they made contact—but they didn't cut the skin any more.

HOCKEY NET

The hockey net was probably invented in 1899 in—where else?—Canada. Hockey players in Nova Scotia threw fish nets over the goalposts to make it easier to determine whether a puck had scored.

MORE THAN FUN

Need to settle an argument, train a warrior, or maybe even cure a person's illness? Play a game of lacrosse! This is what Native North Americans, originators of the sport, would have done hundreds of years ago. Back then, teams of more than one hundred players competed on an enormous field to either put a ball (about the size of a modern tennis ball) between two posts or hit a goalpost with the ball. Players used a one-metre stick made of carved wood. At the end of the stick was a round or oblong "pocket" of dried animal gut that was used to catch and throw the ball. The games sometimes went on for days.

By the mid-1800s, news of this sport, called baggataway, had spread. The French missionaries, who thought the sticks looked like bishops' staffs, or croziers, called the game *la crosse* (the cross). The name stuck. The modern game of lacrosse was invented in 1867, when Dr. William Beers, a Montreal dentist, set out the first rules for the sport. The numbers of players, the size of the field itself, and the length of the game were all reduced. A new lacrosse stick was developed to help players release the ball from the netting more efficiently. A 1994 act of Parliament made lacrosse Canada's national summer sport.

■ Montreal's Shamrock Lacrosse Club, the eventual world champions.

ON AND ON

Hockey continues to be played enthusiastically in Canada, and Canadians keep inventing more ways to improve the game. Canadians have been issued patents for skate-sharpening machines and many different types of ice hockey sticks. Several different kinds of skates have also been patented, including, in 1997, a goalie skate with a "toe-thrusting edge blade."

CROKINOLE

Know how to shoot a marble? In crokinole, you use the same motion to shoot a flat, round puck-like wooden piece from the edge of a circular board into a hole in the centre. You and your opponent each have twelve pieces (also called cookies, buttons, or discs). The trick is to avoid hitting any of the eight rubber-covered pegs that encircle the centre. Fly into one of those and your piece will ricochet into the gutter. But if an opponent has a cookie on the board, you must try to knock it off—and leave yours on.

Wayne Kelly, author of *The Crokinole Book*, says, "Crokinole is indeed a Canadian invention." He notes that the earliest known crokinole board was made in 1875 in Perth county, Ontario. Although the name comes from the French word *croquignole*, which means "fillip" (that is the word for the flicking motion of your finger as it strikes the cookie), crokinole is probably a mix of an old British pub game and a game played in East India. Game historians think that the Mennonites of Southwestern Ontario were the ones to blend the two existing games into this new Canadian game.

■ Wayne Kelly is known as Mr. Crokinole because of his work promoting one of Canada's favourite board games.

ROLL THAT BALL

Although bowling wasn't a Canadian invention, that didn't stop Canadians from enjoying it. But it wasn't perfect—especially if you were trying to play during your lunch hour. There just wasn't enough time to finish a game.

In 1907, Thomas Ryan, owner of the Temperance Street Bowling Club in Toronto, had a solution. After watching his time-strapped customers ask for five pins to be set up instead of the normal ten, he began to go to work. Ryan refined the pins, making them smaller (and therefore easier to knock over) and placing a band of rubber around their middles (to make them less noisy when they fell). He also made the bowling ball lighter, about one-quarter the weight it was in ten-pin bowling, and he changed the rules to allow a player to throw three balls, instead of two. Five-pin bowling became a wild success. Too bad Ryan forgot to patent it!

■ Peg Seller paved the way for today's many talented Canadian synchronized swimmers.

Swimming in Sync

The goal of the Royal Life Saving Society (RLSS) was mainly to teach people water-rescue techniques and thereby reduce the number of drownings. As early as 1896, formal lifesaving classes were being in taught in Toronto. Other branches of the RLSS soon sprang up across Canada, and Canadians were taking to the water to learn how to save lives and how to swim well themselves. A swimmer had to be able to perform special strokes and tricks before he could obtain an RLSS diploma.

Then along came the Canadian women. As they worked to achieve their RLSS diplomas, they enjoyed the challenge of perfecting and combining their strokes. In 1924, a "fancy swimming" competition was organized in Montreal. Twenty-year-old Margaret Shearer, later known as Peg Seller, helped write the rules for the competition, won it, and went on to turn "fancy swimming" into a popular worldwide sport!

For many years, male and female performers in Europe, Australia, and North America had been putting on dance displays in the water, and there had even been some competitions. But none of this was being done to music, and there weren't any standardized rules.

That was soon to change. Seller, who also excelled at diving and water polo, began to work with other avid female swimmers to organize swimming shows to music. Sometimes in these performances, groups of swimmers swam together to the beat of music in a synchronized way. Spectators were impressed, and an interest in these shows began to grow across North America.

In 1938 Seller established standards for judging "fancy swimming," and by the 1940s competitions were reflecting these standards. Music became compulsory, routines were added, national competitions were established, and the name of the sport was changed to synchronized swimming. Seller went on to institute six Canadian championship events in the late 1940s, establish the Canadian Amateur Synchronized Swimming Association, and write the rules governing international competition. Through her pioneering efforts, synchronized swimming was introduced as an exhibition sport at the Olympic games in 1952. It became an official women's event in 1984.

ZAK ATTACK

Ever played with Zaks? There's a good chance you have, because this construction toy is internationally popular, an award winner ... and, oh yeah, it was invented by a Canadian, James Zeigler.

HOCKEY AT HOME

Donald Munro built the first table hockey game in the basement of his house in the early 1930s. Each player twirled a paddle, which moved five "skaters" who were trying to shoot a steel ball into the opposing team's net, which was protected by a pivoting goalie. Munro made the game so that it was tough and unbreakable. If you lost the steel puck, you could simply replace it with a marble, and if a wire bent or broke, it could be replaced with a piece of wire hanger. Why were the games painted red and green? Munro invented table hockey during the Depression to help raise enough money to support his family, and these were the only colours he had available in his basement!

Donald Munro's Table Top Hockey Game was patented in 1932. His company went on to become the largest manufacturer of table-top hockey in the world.

■ Donald Munro's first table-top hockey game was designed to last.

STANDING TALL

Want to race—on stilts? Just be sure you don't challenge Pierre Blanchard, of Granby, Quebec. An acrobat and mechanic, Blanchard is the proud inventor of the highest stilts in the world. How fast can he go on them? Hold onto your hat—he can reach speeds of up to forty-eight kilometres an hour!

James Naismith

It wasn't an easy childhood for James Naismith. He was born in 1861 in Southern Ontario, but by the time he was nine, his mother and father had both died of typhoid fever. He and his brother and sister went to be looked after by their aunt and uncle, who lived just outside the town of Almonte, Ontario.

Perhaps it was his love of sports that helped James struggle through. He was good at lots of them, including rugby, curling, gymnastics, lacrosse, and football. He also liked ice-skating, but he didn't have any skates and he didn't want to ask for money to buy them. The solution? The enterprising James shaped and sharpened some old wood files, attached them to hickory strips, and then strapped them onto his winter boots. Now he could join in the fun too!

James was bright, but he didn't finish high school until he was twenty-one. That's because he helped his aunt and uncle with summer farmwork and worked for several winters in logging camps. When he did graduate, he was accepted to Montreal's McGill University, where he kept his marks near the top of the class.

After three additional years at a Presbyterian seminary in Montreal, Naismith headed to the International YMCA Teacher Training School in Springfield, Massachusetts. He had decided that teaching sports to young people would be a great way to help them become confident, honest, and fair—all while they were having fun. But once he was an instructor, Naismith found himself teaching a gym class of bored students. They weren't boys, but instead were men in their twenties and early thirties who were training to be YMCA directors.

It was winter—too late for football and too early for baseball—so how was Naismith to capture the interest of his grumpy students? He tried adapting outdoor games for indoor

No one-sport wonder, James Naismith also invented the football helmet!

Basketball was an instant hit, and its popularity quickly spread.

play, but none of them were popular with the men. There seemed to be only one solution: he would have to invent a completely new game, a game that was made for playing indoors.

Undaunted, Naismith thought back to the many games he already knew. He remembered a childhood game, Duck on a Rock, in which players tried to knock a rock off a bigger rock with a stone. He also remembered a rugby exercise that involved throwing a ball into an empty basket. What if he combined the two ideas but changed them slightly?

In December 1891, he cleared the gym of all the climbing ropes and rings that usually hung about. When the students entered, they were surprised to see two peach baskets nailed to the balconies at each end of the gymnasium. (Why peach baskets? Apparently, Naismith had wanted to use boxes, but peach baskets were all that was available at the school.) Because Naismith wanted his game to be non-contact, he had decided to put the goals up high. His reasoning was that if they were out of reach, this would eliminate the usual body contact players used to protect the goal. Also, in a flash of inspiration, he had decided that if players were not allowed to run when

carrying the ball, as they did in football, this would eliminate the need for tackling.

The men read the thirteen rules that Naismith had prepared and pinned to a bulletin board. Then they began to play. The game was a hit right from the start. Of course, there were some changes made along the way. The players got tired of going up to the balcony or using a ladder to retrieve the ball from the basket. Eventually, the bottoms of the baskets were cut out so the ball could fall right through.

Such a great game had to have a name, but James Naismith refused to name it Naismith Ball. In the end, a student suggested the name basketball, and that's what it has been called ever since. Very quickly, basketball became the hottest new sport around—and it is still extremely popular today. But interestingly, Naismith himself only played it twice, in 1892 and 1898. After all his years of rugby and football, apparently he found it too hard not to use body contact. He made too many fouls!

The first basketball team, 1892.

This early game shows how the sport got its name.

When Naismith was in high school, the typewriter and the telephone were invented. While he was attending university, the first gas-driven car was built—although it had only three wheels!

QUESTIONS AND ANSWERS

In December 1979, Canadians Chris Haney and Scott Abbott were bored with their jobs. The two friends decided they would try to come up with a popular game and maybe make some money selling it. It seemed natural to the two journalists to invent a game that would require the players to answer questions based on why, where, when, who, or what. In less than an hour, sitting around the kitchen table, Haney and Abbott came up with the basic concept for the game. They decided to call it Trivia Pursuit, but Haney's wife advised them that Trivial Pursuit sounded better.

Soon the men had formed a company and were manufacturing and selling the games. Word got around, and by late 1983, 3.5 million games had been sold. Now sales are over $1 billion. Trivial Pursuit is sold around the world, in eighteen different languages and in different versions. It is one of the all-time leaders in board-game sales. And it all started with two guys sitting around a kitchen table …

■ The original Genus edition of Trivial Pursuit.

BATTER UP?

Is baseball an American or a Canadian invention? Here's Bill Humber, a Canadian sports historian, on the subject: "Americans have long claimed that baseball was invented in Cooperstown, New York, in 1839 by Abner Doubleday. We now know that a game of early baseball was played in Beachville, Ontario, on June 4, 1838."

So clearly this means that baseball was invented in Canada. Or does it?

"Baseball evolved from spring celebrations practised thousands of years ago in northern Europe," explains Humber. "In the 1700s, a baseball-like game called rounders was being played in Britain. It came to North America and developed through regional variations. These included the New York game, the Massachusetts game, the Philadelphia game, and the Canadian game. Of these games, the New York game, developed by Alexander Cartwright and others, was the successful experiment. It became baseball as we know it today."

So which is it then? An American or a Canadian invention?

"It's more correct to note that no one invented baseball," says Humber.

And there you go! What do you think?

3D FUN

Jigsaw puzzles were first invented about two hundred years ago, and they hadn't really changed all that much until Paul Gallant came on the scene. One day in 1990, the Quebecer jotted down some ideas for how to add a third dimension to traditional jigsaw puzzles. Suddenly, he had the answer: create puzzle pieces that are flat, irregular-shaped "blocks" that can interlock. He even figured out a way to shape their joints so that they would form a flat plane and could also join together to form edges with vertical pieces. The puzzle could stand up on its own!

In 1991, Wrebbit Inc. was formed to manufacture the puzzles in a garage in Montreal. The first of many Wrebbit puzzles was the Old Mansion, based on an 1876 Victorian mansion in Montreal. Since then, many others have been designed, from totem poles and igloos to the *Titanic*. The garage was left far behind as the company expanded. Now Wrebbit exports 3D puzzles in many designs to more than sixty countries around the world. Jigsaw puzzle fans certainly owe a lot to Paul Gallant!

■ Wrebbit and Paul Gallant gave the jigsaw puzzle a whole new dimension.

41

SHOE ON THE RUN

Running shoes that can make you run faster? Can there be such a thing? Well, yes, according to the inventors of the high-tech shoes, Benno Nigg, James Wakeling, and Darren Stefanyshyn of the University of Calgary. These Canadian researchers, who began developing their prototype shoes in 1992, had two ideas that they thought could help a runner save energy. The first concerned a joint that is located between the toes and the mid-foot. When this joint flexes, it results in a loss of energy. "Our invention uses stiff plates in the shoes to minimize the flexion in the joint," Benno Nigg explains. "This also minimizes the loss of energy. Our experiments showed that the energy savings in a group of thirty-two excellent sprinters was, on average, 1.7 per cent."

And that's not all. Studies had shown that when people run, the muscles and other soft tissues of their legs sometimes vibrate. These vibrations use up some of the runner's energy. So Nigg and his team used special materials to "minimize the negative effects of the vibrations in the muscles," he says. "Our experiments showed the energy savings were up to 5 per cent." Watch for these new high-tech shoes to hit the track soon!

CLOCK THAT BALL!

"It was something I wanted to know. How fast could I throw a baseball?" says Dave Zakutin. His love of electronics led him to the answer.

In his last summer of high school, Zakutin made the first prototype of a speed-sensing baseball. Using the facilities at his high school, he designed a plastic shell and implanted it with an electromagnetic device (which he had also designed). This device could sense when the ball was being thrown and when it was being caught, and it gave a digital readout of the ball's speed.

■ Dave Zakutin with the Rawlings Radar Ball.

Zakutin handmade one or two speed-sensing baseballs a day, building about one hundred that summer. But when he approached Rawlings Sporting Goods, a large American company that makes standard baseballs and other baseball equipment, to see if he could interest them in his invention, the answer was no. It was too expensive to manufacture.

Zakutin let the project sit for a while, then he went back at it when he had to prepare a project for his final year in mechanical engineering at the University of Waterloo. After redesigning the ball, he and some young baseball enthusiasts drove down to St. Louis to meet with the Rawlings executives. This time, the pitch to Rawlings worked, and the company enthusiastically took on the project. Now Zakutin's Rawlings Radar Ball is sold throughout North America—and you don't need to invest in an expensive radar gun to clock your pitch!

"Hello? Is Anybody There?"

Inventions That Communicate

When members of the U.S. National Academy of Engineering gathered in early 2000 to choose the most important engineering feats of the twentieth century, four communications inventions ranked up in the top ten. The engineers listed radio and television as number six, computers as number eight, and the telephone as number nine. (Of course you want to know number one: it was widespread electrification.)

This really came as no surprise. To us twenty-first century folks, it is hard to imagine a time when you couldn't watch a movie with sound, flip a radio dial to hear the national news, or e-mail or phone relatives across the ocean. Over the past two hundred years, Canadians have played a huge part in inventing devices and processes that make it easier for people to communicate and connect—and they continue to do so today. Who can imagine what exciting innovations the next two hundred years hold?

ROCKS ARE HERE

Since the 1700s, there have been countless aids in place to help sea captains navigate the rocky headlands and hidden reefs of Canada's coastline. About two hundred years ago, a cannon was fired whenever the fog hid the harbour near Saint John, New Brunswick. In 1832, a huge tower with a 500-kilogram bell took over the job of warning ships of peril, and in 1850, Thomas Robson was granted a patent for a fog bell. But during a foggy storm, even a large bell could be drowned out and beams from a lighthouse might not be seen.

That's what prompted Robert Foulis to invent the world's first steam foghorn. The giant steam whistle was installed at Partridge Island, New Brunswick, in 1859. It worked somewhat the way a tea kettle's whistle works. Compressed steam generated by burning coal was forced out through a long pipe. The whistle could be heard at great distances. Foulis knew more foghorns would one day be used along the coasts, and he realized the importance of inventing a system that would allow sailors to identify what foghorn they were listening to. He coded the whistle, so that when sailors heard it, they could identify it as the Partridge Island foghorn.

The Foulis foghorn was soon adapted for use all around the world. The original Partridge Island foghorn operated without stopping for 139 years, until 1998. Finally, it was dismantled by the coast guard and replaced by many electronic navigational aids.

■ Robert Foulis: His distinctive foghorns could be heard from far away.

PAPER, ANYONE?

Want to send a letter? For thousands of years, people have been writing on paper. The early Egyptians made it from a reedlike plant called papyrus (which is how paper gets its name). Others made paper from rice or other types of plant fibres.

By the nineteenth century, Europeans were making paper from old rags. This was the process brought to Canada. But when a local printer in Nova Scotia began having trouble getting enough rags to make the paper he needed, Charles Fenerty came up with a great idea. Some say he had watched wasps chewing up wood fibres to make paper nests, and others say he got the idea when he saw pulp accidentally being formed in the grinding blades of the local sawmill. Whatever his inspiration, Fenerty, assuming there were certainly more trees than rags, invented a process for making paper from wood pulp in 1841. The paper shortages were cleared up right away. Unfortunately, by the time Fenerty thought to patent his process years later, others had already had the same idea.

Much more recently, Christine and Alfred Wong have come up with an alternative to wood pulp—and saved some trees in the process. They have built a pollution-free agripulp mill in Alberta. It makes pulp from the straw that most farmers would ordinarily leave to rot in their fields or burn after harvesting their grass, corn, wheat, or rice seeds. The straw pulp can be used to make paper and newsprint—and one day perhaps even biodegradable diapers!

FAR-OFF SOUND

Sound—it intrigued Alexander Graham Bell from the time he was a boy growing up in Scotland. One of his first inventions was a machine that made a noise like a baby crying! When he moved with his family to Brantford, Ontario, in 1870, he began experimenting to understand how sound travelled. He knew that sound waves caused vibrations, and he saw that his voice could make piano strings move.

In 1874, Bell discovered that the sound waves from a voice could also move thin metal disks. The disks, when arranged properly, could connect or disconnect electric circuits. In 1875, Bell and his assistant, Thomas Watson, began building experimental transmitters and receivers, and connecting them with wires. They wanted to see if they could transmit sound by electricity.

One day in March 1876, Bell accidentally spilled some acid on himself. He called out to Watson: "Mr. Watson, come here, I want you." His words were carried into the mouthpiece of the transmitter. The sound waves they produced were funnelled into a chamber, where they made a thin sheet of metal vibrate. The vibrations in the metal disturbed a magnetic field that had been created by a magnet with a coil wrapped around it. This created corresponding electrical signals, which were carried along the wire to the receiver and changed back into recognizable words. And Thomas Watson heard Alexander Graham Bell's words. The telephone (from the Greek *tele*, meaning "far off," and *phone*, meaning "sound") had been invented!

■ Bell's patent for the telephone is probably the most valuable one ever issued.

AND THAT'S NOT ALL!

The telephone was not the last of Alexander Graham Bell's inventions. He went on to invent the metal detector, a system of air conditioning, a phonograph, an artificial breathing device, the tetrahedral kite, and many toys—among other things.

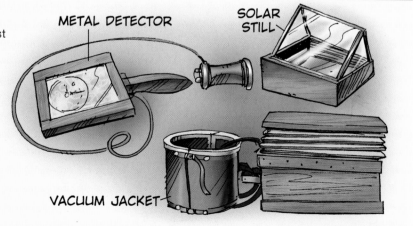

METAL DETECTOR

SOLAR STILL

VACUUM JACKET

DOT, DOT, DASH

Want to send a message or a picture to a friend? Today you can simply fax it or e-mail it. The information—words, numbers, or pictures—is transferred through telephone lines and satellites as a code. Where did the modern data communications system come from? Well, you can trace it back to an idea that a young Canadian had more than one hundred years ago.

In the late 1800s, Frederick Creed, of Mill Village, Nova Scotia, was working in Peru as a Morse code operator. Morse code was a communications system that used dashes and dots in different combinations to transmit letters and numbers. Operators would encode messages by using plungers—one for a dash, one for a dot, one for a space—to punch holes in a long strip of tape. Then they would place the tape into a transmitter, which would send out the code electronically over a telegraph wire. The system worked well, but the tape could be punched only at a slow rate.

So Creed invented a way to speed up this process. Using an old typewriter, he made a prototype of a keyboard perforator. He converted the letters and numbers on the typewriter into their corresponding Morse code signals. When he pressed a key, the combination of dots and dashes that represented that character was punched into the tape.

When Creed sailed to Glasgow, Scotland, in 1898 to perfect his design, the daily newspapers were running foreign news that was already a week old. Transmission of information at the end of the nineteenth century was slow. Soon Frederick Creed was selling his keyboard perforators to clients who were impressed with the invention's ability to speed communication.

Buoyed by this success, Creed invented two more machines. One received transmissions and translated them into a perforated strip. The other, a printer, was used to decode this perforated strip into plain language and print it on ordinary paper tape. By 1913, the Creed High Speed Automatic Printing Telegraphy System was being used to transmit entire newspapers from London, England, to other major centres in Europe, and soon Creed teleprinters were being sold around the world.

■ Frederick Creed's original Morse keyboard perforator.

FLYING PICTURES

In the early 1920s, William Stephenson, who was born in Winnipeg, Manitoba, invented the wireless photography transmitter. With this invention, pictures could be transmitted by radio waves or telephone lines to anywhere in the world. Newspapers scooped up this new technology, delighting the public, and on December 22, 1922, the world's first newsphoto was published in London's *Daily Mail*. Now readers no longer had to wait to see images of what was going on.

■ Stephenson's wireless transmitter ushered in a new era in photojournalism.

■ Edward Rogers at his home telegraph station, 1922.

ON THE AIR

Edward Rogers was fascinated with radios even when he was a boy. In 1911, when he was eleven, he was on the air with one of the first amateur radio sets in Canada, and by the time he was fourteen, he had built his own radio with wires and tubes and could pick up overseas signals on it! It wasn't long until he started up his own radio station on the second floor of his family's home in Toronto.

Rogers was an experimenter, and he began to wonder if he could solve one of the problems with radio. Radios were run on large, costly batteries, and these often ran out when people were listening to a program. People grew tired of the expense and hassle of always replacing these batteries, so in 1924, Rogers invented a special alternating current (AC) tube that could use the electrical current already available in most homes. Batteryless radios were now a reality!

In 1925, Rogers set up a company to manufacture his tubes and the radios that could use them, and in 1927, he established the world's first all-electric batteryless radio station. It had the call letters CFRB—Canada's First Rogers Batteryless.

was in orbit about 36,000 kilometres above the earth. Two more identical Anik satellites, *Anik A-2* and *Anik A-3*, were launched in 1973 and 1976, just to make backup satellites available in case of problems with *Anik A-1*. The Anik satellites were built to carry radio, television, and telephone signals across Canada.

The Anik satellite had a cylindrical body that spun for stability, just like a top. Its antenna was placed on the one section that didn't spin, so that it could always be directed towards Canada. This antenna picked up low-level radio signals from a transmitting station on the ground. Amplifiers onboard Anik boosted the signals, which had been weakened from travelling so far through space. The signals were then transmitted by the antenna back to earth, where they were picked up by more than one hundred ground stations across the country, boosted again, and then delivered to customers from east to west and south to north. At last someone in Nova Scotia could pick up the phone and speak to a friend in the Yukon. The East Coast words would be carried to a local transmitting station, bounced into space as radio waves, then bounced back down to a Yukon receiving station and sent along to the intended recipient!

Canadian communications satellites continue to be improved. The first series of Anik satellites, known as *Anik A*, have been replaced over the years by *Anik B*, *Anik C*, *Anik D* (the first made-in-Canada commercial satellite), and *Anik E*. In 1996, a solar panel was ripped off the *Anik E* satellite. The *Anik E2* satellite system now carries all of Canada's television broadcast traffic.

JOINING THE NATION FROM ABOVE

In a country as vast as Canada, keeping in touch can be a problem. In the late 1800s, people hoped the Canadian Pacific Railway would help keep Canadians united. By the mid-1950s, they had begun looking to the skies.

The space age was born when Russia put the first satellite, *Sputnik*, in orbit in 1957. Five years later, the Canadian space program began with the successful launch of the satellite *Alouette*. *Alouette* orbited the earth collecting data about a layer of the atmosphere known as the ionosphere. It was hoped that the information collected would help improve communications methods.

Advances in satellite technology were made, and soon more satellites were being launched. On November 9, 1972, *Anik A-1* was launched from Cape Canaveral. Just twenty-six minutes later, the satellite

ANUK OR ANIK?

How did the Anik satellite get its name? A national competition invited suggestions, and then a team of representatives from all parts of Canada met to choose the winning name. Finally, *anik*, the Inuit word for "little brother," was picked.

But when the word was written down on the committee blackboard, it was apparently spelled a-n-u-k. The Inuit delegates chuckled, and explained that in the Inuktitut language, *anuk* means "manure."

MAXIMUM MOVIES

Want to get the real feel for Mount Everest or maybe Canada's North—without actually going there? Well, watch an IMAX film about either of these places, and you'll feel like you've really been!

When Graeme Ferguson, Roman Kroitor, and Robert Kerr invented the IMAX format in 1968, they were thinking big. That's why they called their invention IMAX, or maximum image. They wanted to deliver to movie-goers the most that the eye could see. Instead of 35-mm film, the size usually used for making movies, they decided to use larger film—after all, they wanted to show larger images. But because there were no projectors or cameras for this heavier, larger film, the three film fanatics had to invent them. With the help of others, Ferguson, Kroitor, and Kerr designed a new projector (about the size of a small car) and a new camera (weighing about forty-five kilograms). And just imagine the size of the giant screen needed to show an IMAX film—some are up to eight storeys high.

In 1970, the first IMAX film, *Tiger Child*, was shown at Expo in Osaka, Japan. IMAX was a hit then, and it continues to be popular today, taking viewers wherever the camera can go, from outer space to under the ocean—big time!

■ IMAX movies are so realistic that audience members sometimes get motion sickness.

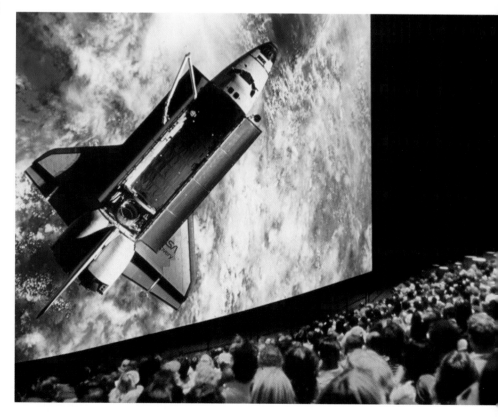

Reginald Fessenden

It would be easy to imagine a cartoon of Reginald Fessenden lying in his crib with a glowing light bulb (the symbol for a great idea) over his head … except that the light bulb hadn't been invented in 1866! Quebec-born Reg just seemed destined to be an inventor. Maybe it was in his genes. His grandfather had designed the first grain elevator and a snowplow for railways. And his uncle was a math and physics teacher who fired young Reg's interest in science.

Reg's parents knew he was bright—perhaps even a child prodigy. Their oldest son was reading everything he could get his hands on by the time he was six. And at eight, perhaps following in his grandfather's footsteps, he built a model snowplow powered by a motor he had put together from clock parts. But the Fessendens hoped Reginald would be anything but an inventor. They wanted him to succeed in the world, and they had seen his grandfather die penniless.

But science and the world of possibilities drew Reginald like a magnet. At eighteen, he plunged full on into the world of inventing when he went to work for Thomas Edison. He loved the work, and sometimes even slept on the floor of the laboratory. By 1890, he had invented a safe electrical-wire covering, an electrical gyroscope, and a new kind of varnish. But he was hooked on the idea of inventing a new type of communication technology—one that didn't need the wires of Bell's telephone.

In 1895, an Italian, Guglielmo Marconi, successfully sent the first wireless message in Morse code over a long distance. Marconi was

Equipment used to power Fessenden's experiments.

sending blasts of energy through the air, starting or stopping them to indicate the dashes and dots of Morse code. Instead of being dismayed by another's achievement, however, Fessenden decided to follow Marconi's lead and find a way to send words through the air, not just codes.

He figured out that it might be possible to send wireless signals as a continuous wave of energy, not just spurts, that could carry words. With this in mind, he went to work to invent a machine that could produce endless radio waves. On December 23, 1904, he was successful. From the wireless station on Cobb Island, Maryland, where he was stationed for the U.S. Weather Bureau, Fessenden performed the world's first voice transmission using the wireless telegraph he had invented. To an associate, Alfred Thiessen, he miraculously transmitted the words "One, two, three, four. Is it snowing where you are, Mr. Thiessen? If it is, telegraph back and let me know."

And he didn't stop there. In 1906, from a station at Brant Rock, Massachusetts, Fessenden was able to successfully complete a two-way telegraph transmission across the Atlantic—the first person ever to send a voice message across the ocean. Radio operators far out to sea must have been astounded to hear a human voice coming over the air waves!

Other firsts followed that very same year. Fessenden was the first to make a long-distance voice transmission over land, and he made the first broadcast from a single transmitter to several receivers. After the sinking of the *Titanic* in 1912, Fessenden invented a way to send waves through the water. He created radio sonar, which used short bursts of sound to calculate the distance from a ship to the nearest underwater object. Sound waves could also be beamed straight down, to determine the depth of the water. And the list of Fessenden's inventions goes on and on. This truly great Canadian inventor changed the world with his incredible ideas.

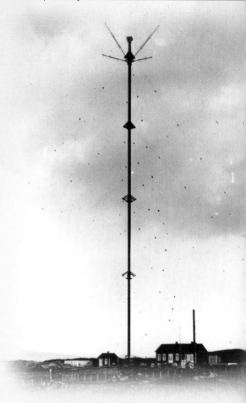

A radio tower antenna, probably at Brant Rock.

Fessenden's associates conduct experiments in wireless telegraphy.

When Alexander Graham Bell invented the telephone in 1876, Reginald's worried parents cut the news out of the paper, hoping their son would not hear about it. But his uncle actually visited the Bells to see how the new invention worked—and then reported all the details of the exciting technology to his delighted nephew.

■ Steve Mann's "wearable computer" evolved from a cumbersome apparatus in the 1970s into what look like ordinary eyeglasses today.

WATCH WHAT YOU WATCH

In 1991, the first prototype of the v-chip (v is for viewer) was made, and as of January 2000, all new televisions made in the United States must have one built in. Invented by Tim Collings of British Columbia, this computer chip for televisions can receive and understand electronic ratings, and can be programmed to block shows with particular ratings. If you don't want to watch violent shows, for example, you can block them from your screen!

MAN OR ROBOT?

He may look like a robot, but under all that technology, he's just a man—a Steve Mann, actually. He was a high-school student in Hamilton, Ontario, when he invented the first wearable computer, and he has been working on, and wearing, "smart clothing" ever since. It may be clunky to wear a computer hard drive, a miniature keyboard, radio equipment, and rechargeable batteries everywhere you go, but there are advantages. For example, Mann replaced the thermostat in his apartment with a radio receiver that could pick up signals from his underwear. He never had to adjust the thermostat again. If he got too hot, sensors turned down the heat automatically.

Mann also invented EyeTap, which looks like a pair of sunglasses but is actually a digital video camera combined with a laser beam. EyeTap is connected to a computer processor that is in turn connected to the Internet, allowing Mann to see the World Wide Web through his glasses. In fact, between 1994 and 1996, you could log on to Mann's Web site and watch real-time video from his EyeTap. That's right! You could see everything that Steve Mann was seeing—from his breakfast cereal to his university lecturers—and you could communicate with him by e-mail at the same time.

Turning Touching into Talking

When Rachel Zimmerman was eleven, she first came across a communication system called Blissymbolics. It used symbols to convey the meaning of words. Non-speaking people could communicate by pointing to the symbols on a Blissymbolics board, but only if there was someone there watching.

When she was twelve, Rachel developed a Blissymbol Printer for a school science fair. "The purpose of the Blissymbol Printer is to allow people who have no other means of communication to share their ideas with the rest of the world," she says. Instead of pointing to the symbols, the communicator selects them on a touch-sensitive board that is linked to a computer. The computer then translates the information into written language. The information can be printed out in Blissymbolics too, with an English or French text.

"The inventing process starts with an idea for making the world a better place," Rachel comments. "Set your goals high, and never give up on your dreams."

Rachel's Blissymbol Printer earned her the right to compete in the World Exhibition of Achievement of Young Inventors.

AND THE ACADEMY AWARD GOES TO...

Movies. They used to be silent, but creative thinking and changing technology led to sound information being recorded directly onto film. Problems with sound still existed, however. For example, when dialogue was recorded on a set, no other atmospheric noise was recorded clearly enough to be used. Much of the other sound on that same track, such as background noise and sound effects, had to be replaced, and music had to be added as well. This meant that many soundtracks had to be edited together, often manually, using many different types of technologies—from tape recorders to video machines to projectors.

Then, in 1991, a Canadian company, Soundmaster Group, was formed. John Scott, Ken Husain, Bob Predovich, and Cameron Shearer, the four men who make up the group, began perfecting their invention, the Integrated Operations Nucleus (ION) system. The ION system makes it possible to weave together soundtracks by linking the old manual technologies with modern, digital computer-based technologies. An engineer in a sound studio can now work up to sixteen different machines from one control surface. John Scott says, "It's like a really fancy, elaborate remote control."

Is the ION system a success? Well, it's being used by Hollywood film companies such as Sony, Twentieth Century Fox, and Disney. And the designers of Soundmaster ION earned an Academy Award for Scientific and Technical Achievement in 1999. That sure seems to spell success!

Computer Speak

When James Gosling met his first computer at age fourteen, it was love at first sight. He loved creating complex things, and writing computer software was a great outlet for that creative energy. He got so good at it that the physics department at the University of Calgary hired him to write software for them. Eventually, he became a student at the university, and after he graduated he went on to study computers at Carnegie Mellon University. He ended up working at Sun Microsystems, a computer company in California.

Gosling's most famous creation is a computer programming language known as Java, which was released to the world in 1995. "It created a revolution in how computer software was written," says Gosling. Java was designed to work on large networks. But most large networks are built from many different kinds of computers. "Most computer languages force you to create a program that runs on just one computer, which makes it very difficult to have programs run all over the network," explains Gosling. "I solved this problem with Java by creating something called a Virtual Machine, which could run on any kind of real machine."

Oh, and speaking of computer languages, let's not forget Tim Bray. This Canadian computer whiz is a proud co-inventor of XML (extensible markup language). But despite its name, it's not really a language at all. "XML is a system that allows everyone to invent their own language to meet their own needs," Bray explains. "These invented languages are easy and efficient to transmit across computer networks across all sort of boundaries—operating systems, database, and human language." Bray hopes XML may do away with some of those traffic jams on the information highway!

■ James Gosling's Java programming language revolutionized the software industry and became the common language of the Internet.

54

Float, Sink, and Roll Along

Inventions on the Move

No one is really sure when the wheel was invented, but it was likely at least 5,500 years ago. Thanks to the wheel, Canadians have been inspired to invent ways to move passengers comfortably and safely in vehicles that roll along rails, roads, and even across muskeg! But why stick to land? As long as people have lived in Canada, they have been inventing new technologies to help them travel across—and under—the water. So get ready to roll as you read about these inventions of land and sea ... and don't forget your bathing suit.

GO!

CAN YOU CANOE?

The canoe was developed over several thousand years by Native North Americans. Although all canoes shared the same basic shapes, they varied in other ways to suit the needs of their builders. A canoe built to withstand ocean waves, for example, was different from a canoe meant to move up a river. People on the West Coast built some enormous canoes, while smaller canoes built for one or two paddlers were more common on interior rivers and lakes. Canoes were also built using different materials. Some were made by digging out the trunk of a tree, while others were sewn together from tree bark. The Native people adapted their invention to suit their needs, the materials available, and their tribal culture. But the basic design that made the canoe easy to manoeuvre with a single-blade paddle needed no improvement.

■ Native women mend a birchbark canoe.

■ Kayaks (above) and umiaks (below)—the perfect inventions for transportation and hunting.

KAYAK AND UMIAK

Canadians have been afloat for centuries. In fact, prehistoric models of kayaks date back thousands of years. These first kayaks were developed by the ancestors of the Inuit, and were used to hunt on seas and lakes. They had a framework of whalebone or driftwood and a flat bottom. Except for the opening where the hunter sat, the kayaks were completely covered with sealskins, often six or seven sewn together. The hunter, clothed in a waterproof suit, gathered the edge of the sealskin around his waist with a belt or attached it to the rim of the cockpit. Now the kayak and the hunter were both completely waterproof.

Steering with a double paddle, the hunter could right himself if the kayak tipped. The kayak could enter very shallow water, could be manoeuvred easily, and was light enough to lift and carry on land. Sometimes hunters actually carried a small sled on the back of the kayak. If they had to cross a lot of ice to reach a good hunting spot, they would load the kayak onto the tiny sled and pull it!

Another boat, called an umiak, was in use at the same time. Like the kayak, the umiak was made with sealskin, but it was open and wide. The stable boat was used for hunting whales or for carrying people and their belongings across wide stretches of open water. The owner and head of the boat would steer from the stern while the passengers paddled. Sometimes a mast was put up and a sealskin sail was raised.

John Patch, inventor of the screw propeller.

CRANK IT UP

Years after the kayak and umiak first cut the waves, wind began to propel great sailing ships across the oceans. Soon the hand-powered paddle gave way to a steam-driven paddlewheel. But John Patch, of Yarmouth, Nova Scotia, believed that paddlewheels were inefficient and awkward, and he was sure there was a better way to move boats. Patch thought about how paddles were sometimes manipulated in figure-eight patterns to propel small boats, and he decided to try to create a machine that would do something similar.

In 1833, Patch attached his handmade propeller to a small boat. He began to turn a hand crank, which was connected to the propeller by wooden gears. Sure enough, the boat began to move! A year later, Patch tried his machinery on a larger boat, the *Royal George*. Once again, he was successful. The energy of the crank worked on the propeller blades to push the boat through the water.

This propeller, known as a screw propeller, revolutionized ocean travel. Paddlewheelers had been taking as much as a month to make ocean crossings, but ships equipped with the new screw propellers could make transatlantic voyages in about ten days. Unfortunately, Patch never got the patent for his invention because many people in other countries were working on similar designs, but he is recognized as the Canadian father of the screw propeller.

ROLLING ACROSS THE WAVES

Imagine a floating cylinder that can revolve around an inner fixed passenger cabin, two engines, and some paddlewheels. You've pretty much got the Roller Boat! Frederick Knapp, from Prescott, Ontario, thought his design would cut down on seasickness because the boat would roll over the top of the water instead of bouncing up and down on the waves. On September 8, 1897, Knapp tried out the prototype in the Toronto harbour in front of huge crowds. On flat water, it went about eight kilometres an hour instead of the expected forty or fifty, and on rough water it couldn't be controlled. The Roller Boat, although remarkable to look at, was a clunker.

■ The doomed Knapp Roller Boat in the Toronto harbour, 1897.

Oiltankers carry hundreds of thousands of litres of oil across the oceans, and when they leak or spill, it can be a disaster. In 1970, Richard Sewell invented the environmental Slicklicker. This portable machine was mounted on a boat and used an inflatable plastic boom to trap spilled oil. A cloth conveyor belt, soaked in oil, was then circulated through the boom. The oil on the belt attracted the oil on the water and soaked it up. The oil from the spill was then wrung out into oil drums and the damage to the environment was greatly reduced. The oil slick was "licked" by the Slicklicker.

BELL (AGAIN!) AND THE HYDROFOIL

Yes, you're right. Alexander Graham Bell has already appeared in this book. Just flip back to page 45 and check out how he invented the telephone. There's even a sidebar on that page mentioning some of his other amazing inventions. But we couldn't resist adding another few paragraphs on Bell's hydrofoil.

In the summer of 1908, Bell and his colleague Casey Baldwin began puzzling over how they could build a boat that would lift out of the water and travel on "skis." They believed a boat that could do this would go faster than one whose hull had to drag through the water. By 1911, they had built the HD-1, what they called a hydrodrome. It was a boat, but it looked more like a little seaplane! The HD-1 rested on hydrofoil plates, or blades. When the boat was in motion, the blades lifted, acting in water as airplane wings do in air. As the boat picked up speed, the hydrofoils lifted up until the bottom of the hull was above the water. Bell was thrilled to observe that the reduced drag did indeed let the boat go faster—as fast as eighty kilometres an hour!

Over the years, Bell and Baldwin made many more design improvements to increase the speed of their craft. In 1919, the inventors completed their final hydrodrome, the HD-4. On September 9, with two 350-horsepower engines powering two airplane propellers, the HD-4 reached speeds above 113 kilometres an hour, making it the fastest boat in the world for ten years! In 1922, when he was seventy-five, Alexander Graham Bell received a patent for the hydrofoil. It was just one year before his death.

■ Bell worked on many of his inventions, including the hydrofoil seen here, at his home in Baddeck, on Nova Scotia's Cape Breton Island.

SAIL AWAY

Strap it to the top of a car, drive to the lake, unload it, and get it in the water. The Laser is a small fibreglass dinghy designed by Bruce Kirby and built by Ian Bruce in 1969. Hans Fogh made the sail. Although it was turned down by the retailer the men had designed it for, they hand-built the boat and its sail anyway, and raced it in a regatta in 1970. The swift Laser turned heads and was soon being produced in Quebec. The sailboat quickly became wildly popular because of its size, its low cost, and its easy handling. Now more than 175,000 Lasers have been produced and sold in more than one hundred countries. In fact, this sailboat became so popular that in 1996, Laser sailing was recognized as an official Olympic water sport!

■ Easy to use but speedy and fun, the Laser is popular with all kinds of sailors, from kids to seasoned veterans.

A WORK IN PROGRESS

Matthew Garvin, from Portugal Cove, Newfoundland, is perfecting an invention designed to reduce the drag on a boat's hull. In 1999, the nineteen-year-old constructed several different hulls from high-density foam and fibreglass and had them pulled through the towing tank at Memorial University in Newfoundland. Air was then blown through a grid of small holes drilled in the bottom of the hulls.

And what did he learn? "When the hull is moving at high speeds, the air forms into a smooth layer around it. This reduces the friction between the hull and the water. A boat would be able to go faster while using less fuel."

Garvin admits that the mechanism for injecting the air was oversimplified for experimental purposes and needs further work, but who knows? If he can find a way to improve it, he hopes to patent his invention. And one day, sport boats may be cruising the water on a cushion of air!

PATENT PENDING

Ever wanted to dive with wings? Well, take a look at the towed underwater flying craft invented by Dak Conklin. A boat pulls the craft through the water. The rider, balanced on a belly board, tips the wings to move along the surface or dive under water. By lifting one wing and lowering the other, an adventurous rider can even twirl under water. Maybe by the time you read this, the Canadian patent will have been approved for this invention. Don't forget the air tanks!

GOING DOWN, WAYYY DOWN

Gino Gemma remembers how it all began. "A Vancouver salvage company was looking to purchase a small submersible that would allow them to go deeper under the water and stay [down] longer. However, they found out there were no small subs available." The solution? Get someone to build one. A representative from the company met with Mack Thomson in a café, and moments later he was sketching a drawing of the submersible on a napkin. A partnership was formed.

Thomson, an American diver who later became a Canadian citizen, moved to Vancouver and began hand-building the sub with a team of craftspeople. Soon Gemma, a scuba instructor, heard of the project and asked to come on board. By 1967, the world's first commercial deep-diving submarine, or submersible, Pisces I, had been built. It was a two- or three-person vehicle that could dive to almost four hundred metres. And then came Pisces II, Pisces III, and on up to Pisces

XIV. Gemma says, "It's no wonder Vancouver became known as the submarine capital of the world."

It's no wonder, indeed! In 1984, Deep Rover, the most advanced single-person submersible at the time, was designed and built jointly by Can-Dive Services Ltd. of Vancouver and Deep Ocean Engineering Inc. of California. Deep Rover is shaped like an acrylic sphere and has remote-control hands. It can dive to about 910 metres and stay under for four to six hours. It is still in use today.

Deep Worker 2000, which can descend to six hundred metres, was designed by Phil Nuytten in the late 1990s. Pilots steer the tiny crafts with their feet, and they can manoeuvre the arms to perform many undersea functions. Want to hop aboard? These submersibles are now being used by tourists to view undersea shipwrecks!

The Pisces submarines are the ancestors of today's deep-water submersibles. Those vehicles are taking people where no one has gone before.

THE NEWTSUIT

Phil Nuytten, designer of the Deep Worker 2000, also created the Newtsuit. This amazing 315-kilogram suit can be worn by divers at depths of about seven hundred metres. Because of the suit's unique joint system, it gives the diver wearing it almost as much flexibility of movement as he would have in a regular wetsuit.

DAISY SIGHT

Many other underwater inventions keep floating to the surface. In the late 1980s, the basement experiments of Donald Knudsen, of Perth, Ontario, led to the world's first practical underwater digital acoustic imaging system (or Daisy). This award-winning and highly sophisticated technology provides quick and clear visual images of underwater objects.

Elijah McCoy

Have you ever heard the expression "the real McCoy"? People use this phrase when they want to make sure something isn't an imitation or a copy. When they want "the real McCoy," they want the original or the genuine product.

Well, it is very likely that it was a Canadian who inspired this phrase. In 1837, George and Emillia McCoy, two black slaves from Kentucky, fled the United States and slavery. They journeyed all the way north to Canada and freedom. Shortly after arriving in Ontario, George McCoy enlisted in the army, serving in the 1837 Rebellion. When he was discharged, he was given 160 acres of land in Colchester, Ontario, for his service.

The McCoys began working their farm and soon started a family. On a spring day in the early 1840s, the fourth of what would eventually be thirteen children was born. The McCoys named their son Elijah. By the time Elijah was four, his parents knew he was very intelligent and had quite an imagination. He loved watching trains, and was fascinated with the machines and tools on the family farm. His parents had to be patient—Elijah loved taking things apart and then trying to put them back together again!

While Elijah was still a boy, his family returned to the United States. They settled near Ypsilanti, Michigan, where his father began work in the logging industry. Elijah attended the local public school until he was fifteen. During this time, his interest in machines never faded. In fact, it only grew—and it's no wonder. The world around Elijah was changing as more and more machines were being invented and refined. Steam power was moving the engines of the world, and inventors were scrambling to find new ways to harness this power.

McCoy was a kind man who, until his death in 1929, was always happy to open the doors of his factory and show the neighbourhood children his inventions. He told them how important it was to get a good education, and he urged them to stay in school.

An 1882 version of McCoy's Lubricator Cup (left) and a more refined version from 1898 (right).

In 1859, confident in their teenage son's abilities and persuaded by his passion to learn, the McCoys agreed to send Elijah to Edinburgh, Scotland, to study mechanical engineering. Six years later, he returned to the United States, ready to work. The railway was an industry in which a qualified young man would surely find a job—but Elijah faced brutal discrimination. No one would hire a black man as an engineer.

But McCoy refused to give up on his dream. He found work as a fireman on the Michigan Central Railroad. What job was assigned to this bright, creative thinker? Shovelling coal. (At the time, trains were run by steam engines, and the steam was created by burning coal.) McCoy also had to oil the moving parts of the train every so often. This layer of oil protected the steel from corrosion and reduced the friction of the moving parts. But the train had to be stopped for this task. McCoy actually had to jump out of the train and run up and down the length of the engine, applying the oil. Stopping a train and starting it again was not very efficient, and it slowed down every railway journey.

You can imagine how exhausting—and how boring—McCoy must have found this job to be. After two years, he had had enough. He also had many original ideas. He decided to set up a workshop where he could experiment when he was not on the railway. He knew there had to be a way to keep those engine wheels rolling while the parts were oiled, and he was determined to find it!

After trying out and abandoning many designs, McCoy hit the jackpot and patented his first invention in 1872. It was called the Lubricator Cup. This device was a tiny container filled with oil. It dispensed oil from a spigot, but the flow of oil was regulated by means of a stopcock, which was controlled by the pressure of the steam from the engine. The Lubricator Cup oiled the moving parts of the train while the train was running.

McCoy's invention revolutionized the machine industry. Railways, mining operations, and factories that relied on powered machines were able to save time and money by keeping their machines going while they were oiled. And there were fewer breakdowns due to overheating.

Within ten years, every railway engine in North America was using a McCoy lubricating device. Of course, there were imitations that didn't work nearly as well as McCoy's own device. The railway companies wanted the best, and so their employees might have asked for "the real McCoy." Could this be where this now common expression was first used?

McCoy's original patent, granted on July 23, 1892.

With the success of his invention, McCoy was able to quit his job on the trains. In 1882, he moved to Detroit and began to do consulting work for local firms. And he never stopped working on his own inventions. He was granted more than fifty patents in his lifetime, and he believed his greatest invention was his graphite lubricator, which he patented in 1916. It used powdered graphite suspended in oil to lubricate the cylinders of so-called superheater train engines. In 1920, Elijah McCoy established his own company to develop and sell his inventions: the Elijah McCoy Manufacturing Company.

YAWNING ON WHEELS

Have you ever slept on a train? It's very uncomfortable to have to sleep upright in the same seat you have been sitting in all day, but for many years that was the only choice on a train. Then, in 1857, Samuel Sharp invented the sleeper car. Sharp was the first master mechanic of the Great Western Railway in Hamilton, Ontario. When he learned that the Prince of Wales was due for a visit in 1860 and would be travelling by train, he got to work. He designed special seats that could be flipped down at night to become beds. It was very convenient to use one of these coach/bed seats. You didn't have to move to a separate compartment to sleep at night!

The prince certainly enjoyed the special sleeper car seats, and the general public was keen to experience the same comfort. The Great Western Railway began producing sleeper cars, but when George Pullman, an American, copied the design and was able to produce and sell them more cheaply, the Great Western began purchasing the cars from him. Now these dual-purpose cars are known the world over as Pullmans, instead of Sharps.

A crack or a fissure in a steel railway track could result in a serious accident. Unfortunately, cracks were all too common in the early 1900s. The general belief was that they formed because of the high temperatures of the rail-making process. These tiny cracks became larger and more serious with the huge weight of train wheels pounding across the steel rails again and again. But Cameron Mackie, a metallurgist working in Sydney, Nova Scotia, discovered that the cracks were really formed during the rapid cooling period of the rail-making process. He figured out how to slow down the cooling of the rails, and in 1931 the first shatter-free railway tracks were produced. The "Mackie process" was soon being used to make most rails around the world.

■ Samuel Sharp's revolutionary Great Western Railway sleeping car.

ROLLING ALONG

The streetcar rolled to a stop. Passengers jumped off, new ones jumped on, and the streetcar again moved along the tracks. But this was 1880, so it wasn't being powered by electricity: horses pulled the car along the rails. Sure, electricity had been tried, via a power rail buried in the ground beside the track, but it was more reliable to count on a horse. This was Canada, after all, so rain and snow routinely short-circuited the rail.

In the mid-1880s, J. J. Wright and an American colleague showed how wires could be run overhead along trolley poles, and so wouldn't be as susceptible to the weather as the underground tracks. The moving car would be connected to the wires through a pole attached to the roof. The streetcars ran more reliably.

This incredible new power system was shown to the public at Toronto's Canadian Industrial Exhibition (later known as the Canadian National Exhibition, or CNE) in 1883. Thousands tried it out and liked it. After improvements were made, the finished product successfully hit the streets. Soon these streetcars were adopted by major cities all around the world.

There was still one major problem: winter cold. So Thomas Ahearn, of Ottawa, invented a way to keep passengers warm during even the coldest days. He designed and installed the world's first electric car-heating system. A water boiler was placed at each end of the streetcar. Coal heated the water, which then ran underneath the seats in pipes, keeping passengers warm and cozy. Ahearn didn't stop there. He also invented an electric rotating brush to sweep the streetcar tracks clear of snow.

■ This creative fellow, Thomas Ahearn, patented eleven inventions between 1891 and 1921. Busy guy!

OFF-ROAD WHEELS

Maybe you've seen those popular ATVs (all-terrain vehicles) being driven across fields in the summertime. They are certainly a great way to travel across any type of terrain—snow, rocks, mud, swamp, muskeg, desert, and yes, even water! The very first ATV was called the Jiger. This two-person vehicle had balloon-like tires that were blown up with old-fashioned lung power. The Jiger was first produced in 1962 by its Manitoba-based inventor, John Gower. Because of its versatility, it was popular with ranchers, miners, and loggers. Soon many other Canadian companies began producing off-road vehicles, and an industry was born!

SAFETY ON WHEELS

If he hadn't have been wearing his bicycle helmet properly, Gina Gallant's little brother would have been killed when the car struck him in 1998. That's when this young inventor from Prince George, British Columbia, knew she had to do something to make sure all children wore their safety helmets properly.

Gina got the idea to make a helmet that would alert parents and children when it wasn't properly worn. She used the library to read up on electricity, diodes, wires, switches, and soldering. Then she made a prototype using her sister's old helmet. "I made a lot of mistakes," the thirteen-year-old admits, but she never gave up.

Her final patented product "is a combination of light-emitting diodes [LEDs] and switches precisely placed so that when the helmet is being worn properly, the LEDs go on." One of the LEDs is visible to the helmet wearer and the rest are visible to the parent. "If the LEDs flicker or go out, this alerts the child and the parent that the helmet isn't on properly," Gallant explains.

■ Young inventor Gina Gallant and her "smart" helmet.

"There are billions of tires in stockpiles around North America," points out Bob Bryniak, president of EWMC International Inc. "Most companies shred the tires and try to do something with the material, but this is very costly. Other companies burn the tires and use them as fuel. But you are still getting a lot of pollution, and it is expensive to buy scrubbers to clean the air."

The solution? In the 1980s, Dr. Les Emery started experimenting with a process that came to be called reverse polymerization. He discovered that he could break down a tire's molecular structure into its original components: oil, steel, and carbon black. Dr. Emery did his original testing in a little pizza oven that is still in the yard of EWMC.

Today EWMC resells the valuable carbon black for use in photocopy machines, fax machines, asphalt, and new tires, and it recycles the steel. "And we can actually use the energy that we get from the oil to run the very machine that recycles the tires," concludes Bryniak proudly. "On top of that, we get extra electricity from it!" You might just say that these wheels have come full circle!

Up in the Air

Inventions That Fly

When a country is as vast as Canada, there is a lot of sky to behold, so it's no surprise that Canadians have been inspired by looking up. Their hard work and creative ideas have resulted in amazing inventions that have been taking us into the air and even beyond. So strap on those flying goggles and grab a space helmet (just in case), as you take to the sky with these fine examples of Canadian ingenuity.

OVER THE TREES

What do you need to fly above trees and land on small lakes? A Norseman. The Norseman was the first successful Canadian-designed aircraft built for use in the rugged North—and the first Canadian-designed plane to find a market outside of Canada. This single-engine plane was designed by Robert Noorduyn in 1935 in Montreal. It could carry heavy loads, and was able to fly in and out of tight spaces. It could land on dry land, snow, or water—using wheels, skis, or floats.

The Beaver, meanwhile, took to the air in 1947. This all-metal bush plane, designed by de Havilland Canada Ltd., could seat seven people and was the first of the STOL (short takeoff and landing) planes. It was known as a "half-ton flying pickup truck," and was named for that hard-working Canadian mammal, the beaver. Eventually, Beavers were being sold to sixty-five countries around the world, and this legendary plane became the most successful and long-lived design in aviation history.

■ *Top:* Some of the designers and builders of the Noorduyn Norseman stand with their plane in 1937. *Inset:* Beaver from an overpopulated area are loaded aboard a Beaver for relocation.

SUITING UP

Normally, blood flows evenly throughout your body, but if you're the pilot of a steeply turning or diving plane, acceleration can force the blood away from your brain and heart, causing you to black out.

In 1941, Dr. Wilbur Franks, a University of Toronto professor and researcher, invented a special flight suit that contained pads filled with water. When the forces of gravity built up, the fluid in the overalls would press against the pilot's body, forcing the blood to keep circulating. The invention, called the anti-gravity flight suit, was a success. Aircraft pilots around the world still wear anti-gravity suits based on Frank's first design, and even the early astronauts wore the suit to counter the gravitational forces they met outside the earth's atmosphere.

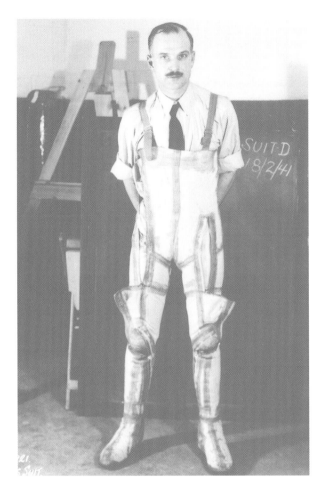

■ Dr. Franks demonstrates his flight suit in 1941.

LOOK HERE!

In the late 1950s, Harry Stevinson, of the National Research Council, came up with a unique way to help locate downed aircraft. He invented the Crash Position Indicator (CPI). This 2.5-kilogram instrument was light enough to attach to even small aircraft, and it had a tough shell of reinforced plastic. It would break free from an aircraft as it was about to crash, land softly, and give out a distress signal no matter where it was—upside down, in snow, or even floating in water. An improved version of this emergency beacon is still in use today. Now flight-data recorders, which give valuable information about the causes of a crash, can be tied into the CPI so that they are easier to recover, and CPI signals can be picked up by satellites, which greatly shortens the time needed to locate downed planes and helicopters.

■ Harry Stevinson and his Crash Position Indicator (CPI).

■ The Avro Arrow in flight: It was faster than any previous aircraft.

THE PLANE THAT NEVER WAS

Another Canadian invention, the Avro Arrow, is famous, or rather infamous, because the project to build these planes got off the ground—and then had its wings clipped in mid-air. Here's the story.

Before the Second World War, aircraft production was not a major industry in Canada. In fact, fewer than one hundred airplanes a year were being built in all of the country. Then, in 1938, with war imminent, Canadian factories began taking orders from Britain to make bombers and fighter planes. Soon, thousands of aircraft were being built every year in Canada—but all except the Noorduyn Norseman were based on British or American designs, and no engines were being produced in Canada.

This was to change. In 1945, A. V. Roe Canada (known as Avro) took over the Victory plant, which had been churning out wartime aircraft. Avro immediately got a contract to build a medium-range jet transport. At the time, it was a very new idea to use jet engines in a commercial transport plane, yet in just four years Avro had built the Jetliner C-102. When the plane flew its initial flight, on August 19, 1949, it became the first commercial jet transport to fly in North America. (It was also only the second in the world, missing first place in the sky by just thirteen days.) In April 1950, it made the first international jet-transport flight in North America, from Toronto to New York.

But then came the Korean War. The Canadian government began to prepare, and this meant re-arming. The government put pressure on Avro to concentrate on producing more of its new fighter planes—and fast. The Jetliner project was abandoned, and the CF-100 Canuck, the first military aircraft wholly designed and built in Canada, went into production.

Shortly after, Avro was asked by the Canadian government to design a new fighter plane that could help defend Canada's North. Two years later, in 1954, the design for the CF-105 Arrow was complete. The Arrow was a supersonic interceptor jet, built to intercept and destroy long-range bombers.

On March 25, 1958, the first flight of the Avro Arrow prototype took place. Over the next few months, more test flights were flown and five more Arrows were built. The tests showed that the jet was faster than any previous aircraft. Many believed that when it reached the production stage, it would be the most advanced, innovative jet interceptor in the world.

Curiously, the Arrow project was halted by the Canadian government less than one year later. Why? Some blame the cancellation on design flaws and excessive costs. And there are many other theories. To this day, however, no one is really certain. One thing, though, is for sure: all plans for the Arrow were destroyed, along with all six existing Arrow prototypes. Sadly, now only a few blowtorched pieces remain.

It's a Bird! It's a . . . What Is That?

Go ahead and rub your eyes, but it's still going to look like a flying baseball! The Ball of Dreams is just one of the wacky spherical airships invented by Ontario's 21st Century Airships Inc. The company has patented several technologies to improve steering because … well, it's hard to steer a sphere!

Wallace Rupert Turnbull

In the 1890s, there were no airplanes as we know them today, but the possibility of flight was finally becoming a reality. Engineless gliders (much like modern hang-gliders) could carry a passenger through the air in a controlled flight. Other designers had connected a propeller to an engine and popped an airplane into the air for a "hop."

But it wasn't until 1903 that the first heavier-than-air vehicle made a sustained, controlled, and powered flight. The plane was flown by two American brothers, Orville and Wilbur Wright, at Kitty Hawk, North Carolina. A gas engine, which they built themselves, and two propellers, which they also built themselves, kept *Flyer* up in the air for fifty-seven dramatic seconds.

How exciting these years must have been! Many, many inventors, not just the Wrights, were hooked on figuring out how to build and design "flying machines" that could stay up in the air longer and be controlled more easily. One man with his eyes on the sky was Wallace Rupert Turnbull.

Wallace Turnbull was born in Saint John, New Brunswick, in 1870. He was bright, worked hard, and wanted to learn. His family was wealthy, and so he was able to pursue his education in different parts of the world. He studied mechanical engineering at Cornell University in the United States and post-graduate physics at universities in the German cities of Berlin and Heidelberg. When his education was complete, Turnbull moved to New Jersey, where he worked at Edison Lamp Works. After six years, he returned to New Brunswick to work as a consulting engineer.

Wallace Turnbull was fascinated with, and had always had many theories about, aeronautics. Eventually, it was not enough for him simply to imagine what could be. No doubt inspired by the exciting developments

Turnbull's variable-pitch propeller was flight-tested for the first time on this Avro biplane in 1927.

in flight, he gave in to his dreams and began to do some inventing.

In 1902, one year before *Flyer*'s successful flight, the thirty-two-year-old Turnbull completely surprised his neighbours by building a wind tunnel—one of Canada's first—in a large barn behind his out-of-the-way house near Rothesay, New Brunswick. A hands-on tinkerer, Turnbull began to test some of his theories there. He tried to design hydroplanes that would lift into the air from water, but after several experiments, he realized that the aircraft engine he was using would never be powerful enough.

Turnbull refused to let his scientific curiosity be defeated, however. He simply refocused, turning his attention to another area of interest—wings and propellers. He knew that the shape of a propeller was as important to an airplane as the shape of the wings, so he added a ninety-metre track to his backyard and placed on it a small wagon to which he fitted an engine. He designed and attached different types of propellers, one after another, and observed and measured such variables as how fast the cart moved and how quickly the propellers turned.

Five years later, Turnbull published his results. He believed aircraft would be more stable if their wings, instead of being straight, were tilted up from their centres to their tips.

This important insight would affect the design of all future aircraft.

Eventually, Turnbull became the leading authority on aerodynamics. In 1916, he began experimenting with the theory of variable-pitch propellers. By then, planes could fly, but they could not get up into the air if they were carrying a load. Turnbull had soon invented a propeller with blades that the pilot could adjust while the plane was flying. In 1923, his variable-pitch propeller was ground-tested at Camp Borden, Ontario, but a fire destroyed a hangar—and the propeller. Turnbull spent two years building another one, this time with an electric motor to control the blades.

Turnbull's new propeller was tested successfully in 1927 on an Avro biplane. Finally, about one year after the black-and-white television was invented, the world's first variable-pitch propeller was successfully lifting an aircraft off the ground!

The propeller functions almost like a car's gearshift.

A close-up view of Turnbull's variable-pitch propeller.

A propeller thrusts the plane forward, so its shape is important. The pitch of a propeller is the angle at which the blades carve through the air. The pitch and the speed of the propeller change the thrust. When a plane is taking off, shallowly pitched propellers give more thrust. But a plane that is cruising needs steeply pitched propellers. Turnbull's invention of a propeller that could change the angle of the blades, or vary the pitch, gave pilots the ability to fly more efficiently.

SPACE ARMS

It took seven years, but in 1981 the Canadarm was finished—and off the ground! The fifteen-metre "arm" had its first trial aboard the second launch of the space shuttle *Columbia*. It was soon being used to launch and retrieve satellites in space, and as a mobile platform for astronauts during space walks.

Developed by scientists from Spar Aerospace Ltd. in Brampton, Ontario, and the National Research Council of Canada, the Canadarm has established this country as a world leader in space robotics. Just like a human arm, the robot arm has joints so that it can swing in all directions. But it also has fourteen kilometres of wiring to carry signals to its parts! It is too heavy to lift its own weight on earth, but in weightless space, the "hand" on the end of the "arm" can lift up to 30,000 kilograms, about the mass of a fully loaded bus. There has been a Canadarm on each space shuttle mission flown outside the earth's atmosphere since 1981.

In 1998, a new robotic arm was built to be used on the International Space Station. (This is the space laboratory orbiting the earth; astronauts will travel from it to the moon, Mars, and maybe even beyond.) This "arm" is called the Space Station Remote Manipulator System, or Canadarm 2.

The new arm is larger, stronger, and more versatile than the arm on the space shuttle. On the end of it is a robotic hand, called the Special Purpose Dexterous Manipulator, or SPDM. The SPDM actually consists of two smaller robotic arms, and these are used for precision work in tighter spaces than the Canadarm 2 can handle. It can slide along the space station on a long track, and it was used to join the station's first two modules, guided precisely with the help of video cameras. (These cameras are part of the Space Vision System, another out-of-this-world technology developed by Canadians.) The Canadarm 2 will also be used to maintain the space station, manoeuvre equipment and payloads, and dock the shuttle orbiters.

■ Thanks to the Canadarm (and the Canadarm 2), we are now known for our expertise in space robotics.

STEM Antenna

Who was Spar's chief consultant on the special gears used on the Canadarm? George Klein, of course. In fact, he had been called out of retirement to lend a hand. The Ottawa-born Klein, perhaps one of the most productive inventors of the twentieth century, invented or helped design a special electric wheelchair for quadriplegics, a microsurgical staple gun, an all-terrain vehicle called the Weasel, and Canada's first nuclear reactor at Chalk River, Ontario.

Klein also had experience with space vehicles. When Canada's first satellite, *Alouette*, was built, George Klein invented the satellite's storable tubular extendible member (STEM) antennas. Four of these special tubes could be rolled up inside the satellite until it was in orbit, and then extended for use. STEM antennas were so successful on *Alouette* that they were used on later manned American space flights, such as Gemini, Apollo, and Mercury, and on many other scientific satellites.

■ George Klein, designer of the STEM antenna, was one of the greatest inventors of the twentieth century.

Space Skin

In 1995, the Canadian Space Agency (CSA) put out a call for help: it wanted to improve the robotic limbs of the Special Purpose Dexterous Manipulator (SPDM). The SPDM had no sense of touch, and that meant that the astronaut manipulating the robotic hand could miscalculate or mismanoeuvre, causing it to crush an object it was holding. Was it possible to develop a kind of robotic "skin" to solve this problem?

Enter Ernie Reimer, of St. John's, Newfoundland, and his company, Canpolar East. Reimer and his team began by trying to copy the tiny pressure sensors in human skin. "Within five months, another team member, Lee Danisch, and I came up with some key insights," recalls Reimer. They invented a new kind of touch-sensitive fabric by embedding fibre-optic sensors in a thin rubber-like material. The scattering of light within the fabric was then used to measure many points of pressure or touch. Reimer and his team members were thrilled. They knew this fabric could cover the SPDM like a skin, sending back tactile data to those operating it.

Reimer calls this "smart fabric" Kinotex. It needs more testing before it can be used in space, but Reimer estimates that it will be part of the SPDM sometime between 2006 and 2011. In the meantime, it has applications here on earth. "The fabric is already being used to make musical instruments and computer touch-input devices," explains Reimer. "Other possible applications … range from games and graphic arts to automotive safety devices, sports applications, health-care applications—just about anything in which the sense of touch can be made to do something useful." Imagine being able to paint a digital picture with virtual brushstrokes or play a computerized guitar with hand gestures!

FLAPPING WINGS AND GUIDING BIRDS

Look! Up in the sky! It's bird, it's a plane … Hey, it *is* a plane! It's an ornithopter, in fact—an aircraft with flapping wings.

"I built rubber-band-powered model ornithopters when I was a high-school student," remembers James DeLaurier, and his interest in flapping-wing flight took off after that. DeLaurier studied to become an aeronautical engineer, and he worked for years at the University of Toronto to develop a remotely piloted engine-powered ornithopter.

Then, on September 4, 1991, after much research, laboratory testing, computer modelling, and flight testing, DeLaurier and his team took their prototype to a hill near Toronto. They started the engines and stood back. The ornithopter took off with several flaps of its wings—and flew successfully and smoothly. "It looked beautiful," says DeLaurier. "In fact, it performed better than my best imagining."

Now let's turn from a plane that looks like a bird to a plane that is followed by birds. In October 1993, Bill Lishman took off from his Ontario farm in an ultralight aircraft that he had designed and built himself for a special purpose. It was to be goose leader to a flock of Canadian geese that had lost their mother and were being raised on Lishman's farm. Just as Lishman had hoped, the eighteen geese followed him and his ultralight, named *Goose Leader*, on a migratory route to Virginia, and the next spring, amazingly, they returned to Lishman's farm on their own, having learned the route from Lishman's unique plane!

■ Like a giant artificial bird, the ornithopter stays aloft by flapping its wings.

Digging In

Edible Inventions

Food ... It's not what you immediately think of when you think of inventions. And in fact, some of the stories included here probably aren't really about inventions. (Check out John McIntosh, for example. In this case, the McIntoshes came across a fruit they spotted as special and worked to make more of it. This is maybe not strictly speaking an invention, but it's a story that is so Canadian, it just has to be included!) But you *will* find here people who have changed a plant to "invent" a new one, have invented a process to produce food a little differently, or have actually invented a new food product. Has your appetite been whetted for more information? Then dig in!

COLD BUSTER

Maybe it's no coincidence that the inhabitants of a land covered in snow and ice much of the year would have a knack for inventing frozen foods. When the Netsilik Inuit, who lived in the Canadian North, were short of wood for their sled runners, they turned to the next best thing—fish! They wrapped fresh fish tightly in a large piece of sealskin and then let the weather do the rest. When the fish were frozen, they strapped them under the sled and off they went, gliding on their newly invented sled runners. And when spring came and the fish thawed, the runners became food once again.

And that was just the beginning for frozen fish. In 1928, Dr. Archibald Huntsman of what became known as the Atlantic Fisheries Research Board invented the first commercial process for freezing fish. Soon Ice Fillets were being marketed across the country.

It all started with ground squirrels. Dr. Larry Wang, a physiologist at the University of Alberta, was researching hibernation in mammals. He noted that ground squirrels in Alberta wake up every so often during their hibernation period, raising their body temperatures to normal levels in four or five hours. To generate the heat to do this, their muscles work very hard—shivering and shaking.

"This aerobic exercise requires the support of fat," says Dr. Wang. "If you and I were lost in the mountains, exposed to the cold, we would die in a few hours—even though we have kilos and kilos of body fat with us! We can't unlock our fat. What do squirrels have that we don't have?"

After four years of clinical trials, Dr. Wang and his colleagues discovered that humans produce a compound called adenosine that "locks up" our fat. They also found that molecules in ordinary food can counteract the effects of adenosine.

Dr. Wang says, "I mixed certain food ingredients to formulate a product that has physiological benefits beyond just calories alone." And voila! In 1991, the Canadian Cold Buster was born. Dr. Wang claims that this patented technological innovation unlocks the body's own fat stores, so that the energy for exercise comes not from the bar, but from the body's own fat stores. The Cold Buster was renamed Access in 1995, and tens of millions have been sold in North America, Asia, Australia, and New Zealand.

■ Dr. Larry Wang shows off his Cold Buster bar. Renamed Access, it's now sold in countries around the world.

An Apple a Day

In 1801, five years after John McIntosh had moved to Ontario, he and his wife began clearing land for a farm not far from the St. Lawrence River. The story goes that the couple found some apple saplings and transplanted them near the new farmhouse. After several years, the trees, each of which was different, grew apples, but they didn't taste very good. Then one day, McIntosh picked a beautiful red apple that had a wonderful sweet taste. Soon all the neighbours were coming for samples.

Allan, the couple's son, learned how to graft cuttings from the special apple tree onto other apple trees, and an orchard was created. The apples were named McIntosh Reds, and by the end of the eighteenth century, they were known all across Canada. Today apples are Canada's most valuable and largest fruit crop—and the most important of all is the McIntosh.

There is now a monument close to the site where the original tree grew. Next time you bite into a McIntosh apple, think of this: the apple you are crunching is related to that first little sapling.

The McIntosh apple is the most important fruit Canada produces.

More Apples

Many types of apples are completely Canadian. Often, they are developed by cross-pollinating one type of apple with another. This way, researchers can choose the qualities they like in two apple strains and try to blend them into one. It's not a quick process, though. "Developing a new apple cultivar can take about ten to twenty years," notes Shahrokh Khanizadeh, a breeder with Agriculture and Agri-Food Canada. "Then it is released to the public for use."

One Canadian cultivar, the popular Spartan apple, was invented at the Summerland experimental farm in British Columbia and released in 1936. More recently, the apple cultivars Nova Easygro (1971) and Novamac (1978) were developed in Nova Scotia. In 1986, the Novaspy apple, also developed in Nova Scotia, was released. It is juicy, ready for picking early, resistant to some apple diseases, and tastes great in pie!

Other success stories include the Blair (1973), Rouville (1983), and Richelieu (1990) cultivars, all developed by Agriculture and Agri-Food Canada researchers in St-Jean-sur-Richelieu, Quebec. In 1996, they also released the Belmac apple. It was named Belmac because the French word *belle* means "beautiful" and there is a "Mac" (a McIntosh) in its ancestry.

But imagine—work first began on the Belmac in 1968, and it wasn't released until 1996. That's twenty-five years! Was it worth all the work? Well, the Belmac grows late in the season, stays firm even after a long period in cold storage, is resistant to scab (the most common disease among all the commercially grown apple cultivars)—and tastes sweet!

BIGGER AND JUICIER

Ever look through a basket of strawberries for that perfect huge one to crunch into? Well, Andrew Jamieson decided he wasn't going to leave it to chance. He is a Canadian plant breeder and research scientist at the Atlantic Food and Horticulture Research Centre in Nova Scotia—and he has been breeding strawberries. In 1998, in fact, he successfully "invented" a new type of strawberry that he named the Cabot. How did he do it?

"I was trying to develop a strawberry plant with large berries," Jamieson explains. "This makes the berries quicker to pick, and so it is easier for growers to get workers to pick them! It also can be easier to sell big berries. Children especially like them. I also wanted to develop a strawberry that would be resistant to several plant diseases, so that growers wouldn't have to worry so much about their plants getting sick."

So Jamieson chose two varieties of berry: one with large berries and one with good disease resistance. "I collected pollen from one plant and placed it on the flowers of another. After the berries developed, the seeds were removed and planted. They grew into 116 seedlings. The best seedling was chosen."

After six years of testing, the new cultivar (or variety) of strawberry was released. The Cabot, which is named for Cape Breton's well-known Cabot Trail, is resistant to many diseases, and its berries are very juicy and exceptionally large—about twice the size of most other varieties.

How does Jamieson like inventing new varieties of plants? "Since I was a teenager, I have been interested in plants. My job as a plant breeder lets me continue this interest while doing work that is useful to others," he explains. "I enjoy eating strawberries very much. In what other job can you get paid for spending your summer eating fruit?"

■ Andrew Jamieson bites into one of his Cabot strawberries. They're enjoyed by young and old alike.

WHEAT HERE, WHEAT THERE

For hundreds of years, Canada has been a great agricultural nation, thanks largely to one crop in particular—wheat. Wheat has been grown in Canada since the early 1600s, and it didn't take long for the country to become one of the world's largest exporters of the product. Today Canada produces more than 50 per cent of the world's wheat and exports about 75 per cent of what it produces. Although there are other Canadian crops that are now very important, wheat is still the main source of income on prairie farms.

But let's return for a moment to the 1800s. That is when you'd find many Canadians inventing implements to thresh, mow, and harvest wheat. And that's not all. They were also changing and improving wheat itself!

In 1820, David Fife moved to Ontario from Scotland. He began experimenting with wheat, and in 1843, he planted some grain sent to him by a friend in Scotland. When Fife's wife, Jane, saw the cows munching their way towards the experimental plot of wheat, she barely managed to shoo them away in time. Only three stalks grew—but that was the beginning. Fife replanted the seeds of the hardy plant and discovered that the wheat grew quickly, produced lots of grain, and made great bread. Over the years, Red Fife became the most successful wheat in Ontario.

Red Fife wasn't suited to the prairie temperatures, however. Charles Saunders, who worked for the government creating new wheat strains, knew this. One day in 1907, he noticed that one strain of wheat, a cross between Red Fife and a foreign variety, had many grains on each head. He chewed on the grains and liked what he tasted. He quickly sent the seeds away for testing.

There was one panicky moment when it was discovered that a worker had taken home the bag of precious seeds by mistake to feed to his chickens! But the seeds were recovered, and by 1908 the new wheat, named Marquis wheat, had proved to be tough enough to withstand early frosts in the West. In addition, it ripened about a week earlier than Red Fife, making it the perfect wheat for the West. By 1909, it was being produced and sold, and eleven years later, 90 per cent of the wheat grown in Western Canada was the Marquis variety.

■ Charles Saunders (left) crossed Red Fife with another variety to produce Marquis wheat (above), which was more suited to the prairie climate.

SWEET THINGS

Canadians have had a taste for sweets for a long time—at least as long as the Ganong family can remember. This St. Stephens, New Brunswick, family has run a candy factory since 1873. In fact, they invented a favourite of Maritimers, the pink Chicken Bone, which has sweet cinnamon candy on the outside and chocolate in the middle. They also are the proud inventors of the five-cent chocolate bar, or so the legend goes.

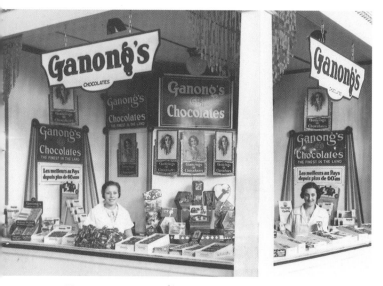

■ A 1934 Ganong storefront in Quebec.

It is said that Arthur Ganong's family had a favourite Jersey cow who wouldn't go into the barn unless she was following Arthur in after his day at the candy factory. The children loved this cranky cow so much that they persuaded their father to take some of her milk and make chocolate from it. Ganong and another candy-maker, George Ensor, added nuts and moulded the small amount of chocolate into long, narrow pieces. The kids were thrilled! Ganong and Ensor made more to take along on their own fishing trips. Finally, in 1910, they decided to market the small chocolate pieces. The world's first five-cent chocolate bar was born.

And since we're on the topic of sweet things, we can't miss out on one of the most delicious Canadian inventions ever to melt in one's mouth: the popular Nanaimo bar. It has a base of graham wafers mixed with coconut, cocoa, eggs, and nuts; a top layer of chocolate; and a creamy, custardy filling. Yum!

Where did this dessert originate? Well, the name certainly came to it from the town of Nanaimo, British Columbia, but the inventor of the recipe still remains a mystery.

Some say that the recipe for the bars came to Nanaimo in the 1850s. At that time, Nanaimo was home to more than ten coal mines. The story is that the bars were sent overseas by relatives and friends in Great Britain as gifts to the hard-working miners. Others believe the recipe was originally brought to Canada by Dutch settlers in the early 1900s. And still others, like Kim Blank, insist that Canada is the true home of the original recipe.

Born in Nanaimo and now a professor at the University of Victoria, in British Columbia, Blank became interested in the origin of the Nanaimo bar recipe a few years ago—when he first decided to try his hand at whipping up some bars. "I asked my mother if she had a recipe for it. Well, she pulled out this well-used old recipe book with an item in it called Nanaimo bars. The book had been put together by a church group in Nanaimo," Blank remembers. "The name beside the recipe was Joy Willgress. I was excited. Was this the first time the recipe had appeared in print?"

While Blank was researching to answer that question, he determined that the story about the bars being sent from Britain to the coal miners was only that—a story with no basis in fact. He also learned that his mother's recipe book had been put together in 1957.

"I did find an almost identical earlier recipe from a Nanaimo cookbook published in 1952," Blank adds. "But the dessert was called Chocolate Slice. The real mystery, then, is when did this treat become called Nanaimo bar, and who was the first person to call it that? So far as I know, Joy Willgress is the first person to put it in print under her name."

And to Blank, this makes Joy Willgress, a Canadian, the proud inventor of the Nanaimo bar.

■ Yellow fields of canola are a common sight in western Canada.

CANADIAN OIL

Rapeseed is a crop that has been grown on the Canadian Prairies since about the 1930s. Its seeds can be crushed to produce an oil, but for a long time people believed that the dark oil was toxic. It wasn't used for anything much more than lubricating machinery, such as steam locomotives and ship engines.

Then scientists and plant researchers got to work. They began trying to alter rapeseed through breeding to create a new type of plant. In 1974, after many years of work, the first canola (from two words: Canadian and oil) plant was developed. Now canola meal is fed to livestock, and canola oil, one of the healthiest edible oils available, is consumed by humans in such foods as margarine, shortening, and cooking oil. It's also used in non-edible products, such as suntan oil, plastic wrap, non-polluting inks, and cosmetics. Canola is now Canada's third-largest cash crop!

GOT THE MUNCHIES?

Just imagine—you purchase a drink, sip it, and when it's done, you nibble on the cup instead of throwing it away! Edible drink containers? That's right. David Aung, a Toronto-based inventor, has come up with an award-winning process for making environmentally friendly containers for drinks. "It's not a breakthrough," he modestly insists. "Think of the ice-cream cone!" Yeah, but on those cold winter days, hot chocolate in an edible cup sounds pretty darn good!

Maple Syrup

Imagine a stack of steaming pancakes and immediately the mind reaches for the sticky maple syrup to pour over top. How was maple syrup invented? Here's one legend: One night, a Native North American stuck his axe into the trunk of a maple tree for safekeeping. In the morning, when he pulled out the axe, a watery fluid began dripping out of the gash left by the blade. The fluid collected in a birchbark bowl resting under the tree. The next day, the man's wife noticed the bowl and, thinking it was full of water, used it for cooking stew. The meat tasted wonderful and sweet! The couple quickly figured out that the container had really held sap from the maple tree.

It wasn't long until Native North Americans invented a way to make syrup from sap. They would collect sap from many trees, take it to a sugar hut, and leave it out overnight. The water in the sap would rise to the top and freeze, and could be easily removed the next morning. After several nights of this, the sap was boiled slowly, and much of the remaining water evaporated. Finally, only the dark sweet maple syrup was left!

When the early settlers arrived in Canada, they began making syrup too. They drilled holes in the maple trees and made wooden spouts, or spiles, to channel the sap into wooden buckets. Time passed and technology changed. Canadians began to use aluminum spiles and buckets. They emptied the buckets

A 1950s sugar hut.

into a gathering tank, which was pulled by sleigh to a sugar hut. A machine called an evaporator made the boiling much easier, but it was still very time-consuming to go from tree to tree, gathering sap from each bucket. In fact, the maple syrup industry could not keep up with the huge demand for the tasty treat.

When plastic tubing came along, syrup producers began using it—and the force of gravity—to carry the sap from high in the tree to a lower collection point. Then in 1970, Denis Désilets and two colleagues, of the Université de Laval in Quebec, learned that if the system of tubes was closed and placed on a steep slope, a natural vacuum was created—and the amount of sap collected greatly increased.

"We began a research project to develop a system using pumps to create an artificial vacuum at the tap," explains Désilets. "This research was a total success. Today, most of the maple syrup produced in Canada comes from a network of tubes tied to vacuum pumps. This can increase the yield by more than 100 per cent, and it allows producers to tap larger and larger orchards."

Tapping a maple tree in Ontario with plastic tubing.

Tarte au Sucre, or Sugar Pie

When the first pioneer families came to Eastern Canada, they likely brought some sugar with them. But it would have run out quickly. They soon became dependent on maple trees for their sweet sap, learning from the Natives how to turn it into maple sugar. They tried to make enough rich brown cakes of sugar to last them all year. That way, they could add a pinch anytime they wanted to sweeten their food. It's no wonder, then, that there are many local recipes that feature maple sugar!

Maple sugar pie, or *tarte au sucre*, was probably invented in French Canada. A Québécois recipe for the pie suggests whisking together $1\frac{1}{2}$ cups (375 mL) of grated maple sugar, $1\frac{1}{4}$ cups (300 mL) of light cream, 2 tablespoons (25 mL) of flour, and $\frac{1}{4}$ teaspoon (1 mL) of pure maple extract. After pouring the mixture into an 8-inch (20 cm) prepared pie shell, you bake it on a baking sheet in a preheated oven at 350°F (175°C). When the filling is set (after about 25 minutes), let it cool first on the counter, then put in the refrigerator to help it set more before serving. Want to jazz up this sweet treat even more? Serve it with whipping cream!

FOOD FOR BABIES

In the early 1900s, Canadian babies were dying of malnutrition. It wasn't that they weren't eating, however; the problem was *what* they were eating. Moms and dads back then didn't know that the finely milled grain cereals they were feeding their babies had little nutritional value. The good stuff—the bran and the germ—was going to the pigs and chickens. Also, porridge was prepared in big batches, and sometimes, as it sat around (remember—there weren't any refrigerators then), it attracted bacteria. When babies were served their meal, they often got sick.

In 1929, at Toronto's Hospital for Sick Children, three concerned nutritionists began to work on developing a new type of baby food. Drs. Theodore Drake, Frederick Tisdall, and Alan Brown developed a biscuit from a mixture of wheatmeal, oatmeal, cornmeal, wheat germ, brewer's yeast, bone meal, and alfalfa. This nutrient-rich biscuit was called Sunwheat.

Sunwheat was perfect for toddlers, who had teeth and could chew on it, but babies were still being left out. So the doctors got back to work. This time, they baked the mixture and extracted a white, flaky powder. When warm water or milk was added to it, babies could easily swallow the yummy mash. The powder was given the name Pablum, from the Latin *pabulum*, which means "food." Since 1930, this Canadian invention has nourished millions of children around the world.

■ The doctors who invented Pablum saved countless lives.

INVENTING RECIPES

Ever thought you could invent a recipe? Nine-year-old Martin Erlic, of Victoria, has been doing it for years. It all started when four-year-old Martin decided to help his grandmother make bread. He really enjoyed pushing the bread dough back and forth.

"I like inventing recipes for my family," says Erlic. "My favourite one is probably Fizza."

Fizza? You heard right, and it's just like it sounds!

"Fizza is a pizza crust with all sorts of fruits for toppings," he explains. "Then I drizzle syrup, whipped cream, honey, or sweet fruit sauces such as banana or strawberry sauce on top. And I sometimes add chocolate sprinkles!"

Erlic has also invented Soy Banana Shake, Bowling Ball Toast, and even Bite the Bark Dust.

POTATO TIDBITS

Many Canadian inventions involve home-grown potatoes. Here are a few:

- You can preserve fruit, and even cucumbers, so why not potatoes? Aganetta Peters, of Manitoba, decided to give it a try. She invented a process that involved peeling and cutting potatoes, placing them in a saltwater solution in jars, and then sealing them. She must have liked the results, because she applied for a Canadian patent and received it in 1920.
- And that's not all! In 1961, Dr. Edward Asselbergs, of the Department of Agriculture, invented a process for making instant potato flakes. Add water to the flakes and heat, and—presto!—you can enjoy a heaping serving of mashed potatoes!
- In 1983, the Shepody potato was invented in Fredericton, New Brunswick. It has become one of the most popular varieties of potatoes to use when making french fries.
- This brings us to another Canadian potato innovation—poutine. This French-Canadian concoction has gravy and cheese curds slathered on top of french fries. No one knows when this tasty treat was invented, but it is believed that it was first enjoyed in either the Gaspésie or Quebec City in the 1950s, then spread throughout Quebec and to other parts of Canada. Now you can order it up in Mexico and Venezuela!

SUPER-POTATOES

Potatoes, like apples, are important to the diet of Canadians. That's why researchers have been working to breed and develop potatoes that can cope with the Canadian climate and resist diseases. In the 1980s, two very special potatoes were developed in Canada. The Shepody potato, invented in Agriculture and Agri-Food Canada's Fredericton, New Brunswick, laboratory, has become one of the most popular potatoes to use when making french fries. And the Yukon Gold, invented by Dr. Gary Johnston while he was at the University of Guelph, in Ontario, is now popular across North America for its delicious flavour and golden colour.

But the hottest potato news comes from the University of Victoria, where two molecular biologists, Dr. Santosh Misra and Dr. William Kay, have invented genetically modified potatoes. These potatoes are designed to grow larger and resist disease, especially something called late blight, which is the disease that devastated potato crops in Ireland in the mid-1800s.

"The widespread famine killed over one million people," explains Dr. Kay. "The disease has been controlled until now with deadly chemical fungicides, but the fungus responsible has become resistant. It is ravaging the world's potato plants, which are an important staple of people worldwide."

So how did the super-potatoes hold up when they were deliberately exposed to this disease? "They remained disease-free, grew larger, and remained succulent longer during storage," reports Dr. Kay.

Now the scientists are doing tests to determine if the potatoes can be safely eaten by humans. "Because these super-potatoes resist the late blight fungus, there is reduced reliance on chemical sprays," claims Dr. Kay, "and this helps the environment. We are also trying to extend our results to non-food plants, such as trees and flowers. We would like to create elm trees that are resistant to Dutch elm disease, a disease which has destroyed much of Europe's and North America's stately elms."

■ The Shepody potato makes a great french fry.

TORTILLAS, ANYONE?

Sure, the tortilla has been around for a long time, but traditionally it has been made of corn. Well, make room for the barley tortilla!

Nancy Ames, a research scientist from Winnipeg, has been trying to find new food uses for barley, a grain that has been used primarily for animal food or malting. "Others have added barley flour as an ingredient to wheat flour," Ames reports. "But our tortillas are 100 per cent barley with no added wheat flour."

How do these nutritious tortillas taste? "Barley tortillas have more flavour than tortillas made from ordinary wheat flour," says Ames, "but my kids think the best thing about them is their texture. Also, because they are soft and pliable, they roll up without cracking and falling apart—which means more room for filling them!"

GIANT PUMPKINS

How big is big? Well, in the 1940s and 1950s, the largest pumpkins were about thirty-three kilograms. Then Howard Dill, of Windsor, Nova Scotia, began experimenting with pumpkin seeds. Eventually, he perfected a strain of seeds that he called Dill's Atlantic Giant. By 1984, Dill had won four consecutive world championships and held the world record with a pumpkin weighing almost 225 kilograms. Now that Dill is marketing his seeds, others have produced pumpkins weighing more than 450 kilograms. Now that's big!

■ Howard Dill's giant pumpkins are many times the size of their creator.

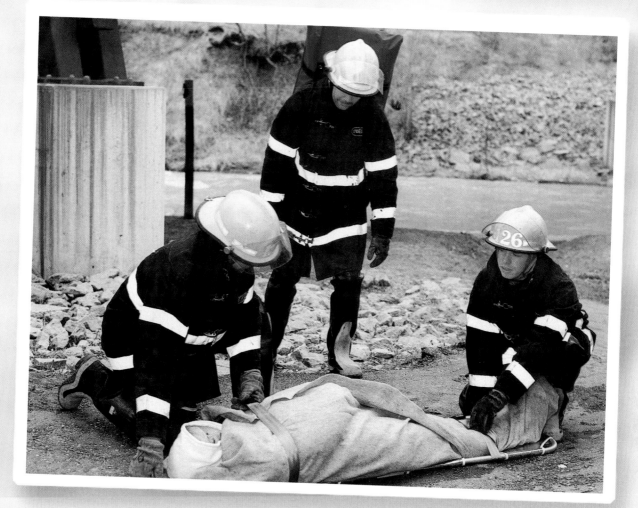

Some Body

Inventions That Meet Physical Challenges

Our bodies aren't perfect. Sometimes we have to face the challenges of a wound, a malfunctioning heart, or the loss of an arm. Many Canadian inventors have sought ways to help us cope with our less-than-perfect bodies. Committed and creative people from Norman Bethune to Wendy Murphy have transformed the materials around them into what they needed to make something work. As technology advances, the range of possibilities broadens. Canadian inventors dream big—and turn those dreams into reality.

■ Dr. Bethune and a colleague stand by one of the vans of their mobile blood service in Spain in the late 1930s.

BLOOD TO GO

When he was eight years old, Henry Norman Bethune found the brass nameplate that used to belong to his grandfather, Dr. Norman Bethune. Henry Norman hung it on his door and decided then and there that he wanted to be called Norman, like his grandfather, and that he wanted to be a doctor, like his grandfather.

Both things eventually happened. In 1928, Dr. Norman Bethune, of Gravenhurst, Ontario, joined the staff at Montreal's Royal Victoria Hospital as an assistant chest surgeon. He soon began improving existing surgical instruments and inventing dozens of new ones. For example, to replace the awkward, heavy rib shears surgeons were struggling with, he invented the Bethune rib shears—and these are still in use today. He also became known for his innovative surgical techniques.

In 1936, Bethune went to Spain, where there was a civil war taking place. He felt he could help most by starting a mobile blood service. This wasn't a new idea, but no one had ever put it into practice before. Instead of bringing the injured to hospital to receive blood, which was a time-consuming process, Bethune collected blood from volunteers, stored and refrigerated it, and took it to the injured on the battle lines. Because they could be helped quickly, more soldiers survived.

In 1938, Bethune travelled to China, where there also was a war. Because there was no way to refrigerate blood there, he could not put into place a mobile blood unit. Instead, he assembled the world's first mobile medical unit. A medical person would travel to the injured with two mules loaded up with equipment. Because the unit was constantly on the move, following the front line, all the equipment had to be light and mobile. In addition to many more surgical instruments, Bethune invented special mule packs to carry all the equipment and even one that opened up to become an operating table.

Norman Bethune's finger was cut while he was performing an operation in China in 1939. Tragically, this well-loved Canadian doctor and inventor died of blood poisoning within the week, at the age of forty-nine.

Da-Dump, Da-Dump, Da-Dump

A regular heartbeat is nothing to take for granted. When a heart begins beating erratically, death may be near. More than fifty years ago, Dr. John Hopps, from Winnipeg, began studying ways to control the heart. He was able to learn from the many experiments that had already been done by other scientists, including a Canadian, Dr. Wilfrid Bigelow.

In 1950, Dr. Hopps produced the first heart pacemaker prototype. By firing electrical pulses at a certain rate, or pace, it could start a stopped heart and regulate the heartbeat. It was combined with a defibrillator so that a heart contracting irregularly could be shocked back to its normal rhythm. This first pacemaker was too big to be implanted in a person's chest, but research continued to modify and improve it. Finally, in 1958, the first pacemaker was implanted in a human. New models continue to be developed today.

And that's not all. Artificial hearts, which maintain blood circulation when a heart has failed, have been in development since at least the 1980s. They originally consisted of large machines that had to be hooked up to patients with heart failure. Now Dr. Tofy Mussivand has invented an artificial heart-assist device, which he calls the Heartsaver. It is an artificial heart that can be implanted in a person's chest either permanently or temporarily (until a transplant organ becomes available). It is powered by a battery pack that the patient wears on a belt, which means he or she can move about and lead a fairly normal life. It can also be remotely monitored and altered across great distances, which means that patients can have access to hospitals without actually having to go to them! So far the Heartsaver has been tried out only on dummies, but it will soon be tested on human patients.

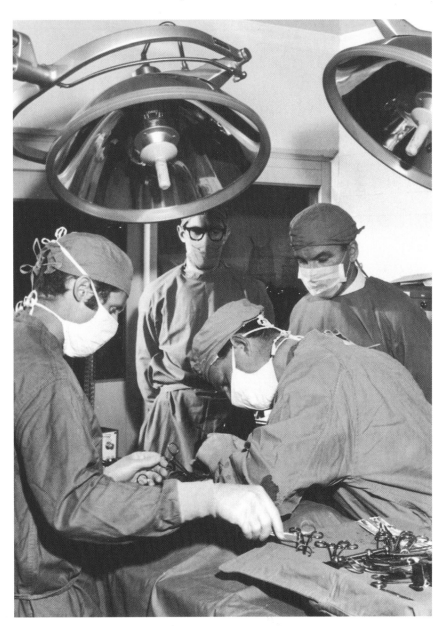

■ Dr. John Hopps in his operating theatre.

TAKE HEART

When Barbara Nowinski experienced enormous pain in her chest area in 1997, she was rushed to the hospital. In the end, tests showed that her heart was fine, but her sons Jack and Mark were left to wonder what would have happened if their mother had suffered a real heart attack.

This prompted the seventeen-year-old Waterloo, Ontario, teenagers to invent an electrocardiograph (ECG) that can be used at home to monitor the heart. The size of a tissue box, the machine can be set up (it hooks up to a home computer) and run in less than thirty seconds. The person being monitored puts three electrodes on his or her body and connects a wire to each one. "After all the physical connections are set up, the software then performs an extensive analysis of the person's ECG signal. If any serious abnormalities are present, the ECG calls an emergency response centre or dials into a doctor's computer. The doctor can view the results in real time and decide what to do," explains Jack.

With this clever invention, there's no waiting around for a diagnosis! And if the person's pulse

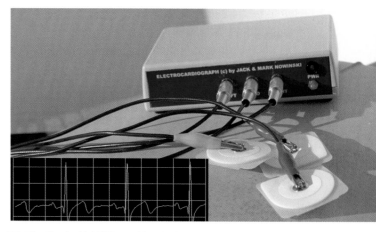

■ The Nowinskis' ECG machine is about the size of a tissue box.

disappears during the analysis, the device has the ability to revive him or her. The software can receive a signal from the emergency response centre and send an electric shock to the electrodes.

The invention has won Jack and Mark many awards at science fairs. "They say necessity is the mother of invention," says Jack. "In this case, mother was the necessity for the invention!"

■ Dr. Thomas Chang's artificial blood cells measure only one millimetre around.

REAL—OR FAKE?

In 1957, when he was twenty-three and an undergraduate at McGill University in Montreal, Thomas Ming Swi Chang invented the world's first artificial cells—tiny, extremely thin plastic capsules that contained haemoglobin. Luckily, he had sympathetic room-mates who didn't mind his turning the residence room into a laboratory full of not-so-nice smells! A few years later, when he was trying to find a practical use for these artificial cells, Dr. Chang invented the world's first artificial blood.

Dr. Chang continues to perfect his inventions. His hope is that this artificial blood, which can be stored for months instead of days and is disease-free, can be used in emergency rooms without fear of allergic reactions. And it would be a reliable supply, doing away with the need for volunteer donations. Dr. Chang's inventions have led to new artificial cell-based approaches to kidney and liver disease, enzyme therapy, and gene therapy, and it is no surprise that he is a recipient of the Order of Canada.

ELECTRIC HAND FOR KIDS

It used to be that kids with arm amputations or congenital limb differences were fitted with hooks. They opened and closed the hook by using shoulder movements to pull or release a cable.

Then along came a dedicated team of researchers, including William Sauter, Colin McLaurin, Ihsan Al-Temen, and Kaare Lind, at Toronto's Bloorview Macmillan Centre. With the help of the Northern Electric Company, the Bloorview Macmillan team designed the first child-sized myoelectric hand in 1971. This was followed by the first electric elbow and wrist-rotator for kids and young adults. Now, instead of a hook, a child could have a more natural-looking hand.

And because the hand was electro-mechanical, the child could control it by using the muscles left in his or her limb. As the child's muscles contracted, the myoelectric hand picked up these electric signals and reacted. Kids as young as ten months could learn to operate it.

This first myoelectric hand was eventually replaced by a range of electrically powered plastic hands, all designed exclusively by Bloorview Macmillan researchers. In fact, this centre is the only site in the world that produces electric elbows and wrist-rotators. And the researchers haven't stopped there. Recently they invented the MyoMicro. This programmable microchip fits inside a prosthesis, or artificial limb, and allows the controls to be adapted to the abilities of the user.

■ The myoelectric hand (above) is so simple that kids less than a year old can learn to use it. Researchers at the same centre invented the MyoMicro (right), a microchip for use in prostheses.

Wendy Murphy

"I come from a family of dreamers and doers," says Wendy Murphy. In her family, it wasn't enough just to dream—you had to act on your ideas. Her father, a member of the Canadian Armed Forces, was a good example of this. He was involved with the development and testing of one of the first American high-altitude flight suits—the precursor to the space suit. (You can read more about the one invented by Canada's Dr. Franks on page 69.)

"My parents told me that if I worked hard, I could do anything I put my mind to. Giving up wasn't an option. If I couldn't succeed one way, I could try it from another direction," she says. "Great training for a future researcher and inventor!"

Murphy became interested in first aid at a young age. In fact, she remembers reading all of her father's military training manuals for first aid and rescue when she was just eight years old. And her interest in babies? Even as a teenager in Owen Sound, Ontario, she loved babies. That's one of the reasons why she headed to the Hospital for Sick Children in Toronto in 1967. Murphy worked there for many years—first as an X-ray technician and then exclusively with babies.

Then, in 1985, an earthquake shook Mexico—and shook up Wendy Murphy, too. She watched on her television as tiny babies were carried away from a crumbling hospital on adult stretchers. "I decided that there had to be a way to transport babies more efficiently," she remembers, "in a way that would keep them warm and secure." She decided to invent a new stretcher—one that didn't waste space in emergency situations.

Murphy worked hard to come up with a design, but then she put her idea away for a

Firefighters test their emergency preparedness with one of Wendy Murphy's WEEVACs.

while. It wasn't until another emergency struck, this time at the Hospital for Sick Children, that she dug out her old plans. A fire had almost forced the infants in the neonatal unit to be evacuated. When Murphy realized there would have been no way to take them downstairs safely, out came her designs! The hospital immediately put in an order for ten stretchers.

In 1989, two years of research and testing began. There were many setbacks and changes, but finally the infant stretcher was ready for action. WEEVAC 6 (the name comes from "we evacuate," or "we evacuate wee ones") is the only emergency evacuation stretcher in the world designed to carry six babies at a time. Two babies are strapped into each of three pockets.

What are the pockets made of? Well, when Murphy thought about pizza delivery bags, a light bulb went on. If pizza bags can keep a pizza warm and dry, she wondered, why can't the same thing be done with babies? After many tests, she decided the material (it's a Mylar-laminated vinyl) was perfect for the pockets. It is waterproof, sturdy, and holds in heat. She also thought long and hard about the stretcher frame and decided to make it out of lightweight aluminum. That way, two people alone can carry a fully loaded stretcher.

Murphy has won many important awards for her invention, including the 1991 National Research Council of Canada Award and the 1992 Manning Award for Innovation. She has also gone on to invent other emergency equipment, such as a unique incubator cover for transporting infants, adult evacuation systems, and special rescue equipment storage bags for the Canadian coast guard's inflatable rescue craft.

Murphy says, "Where others see a list of problems, inventors see only a list of solutions!"

Each WEEVAC 6 keeps six babies safe and warm.

A Real Dummy

When does everyone need a dummy? Well, when they are learning cardiopulmonary resuscitation (CPR), of course. CPR is a series of emergency techniques used to revive someone whose heart has stopped. But it takes practice to learn, and that's where the dummies come in. For many years, CPR was taught using specially designed dummies, but they were expensive and there never seemed to be enough to go around. The Canadian Lifesaving Society approached two Toronto-based industrial designers, Dianne Croteau and Richard Brault, and asked if they could design something less expensive.

"We tried to evaluate what were the essential required elements to perform CPR," remembers Croteau. "The existing mannequin had some pretty complicated parts. We tried to reduce it down to one part. This would allow for the product to be simpler and lot cheaper. We could have ten mannequins for the price of one. Everyone in a class could practice at the same time instead of waiting and watching for their turn." Six years later, in 1990, the Actar 911 was ready for action. This resuscitation dummy is now sold to fifty countries around the world.

■ Canadian-designed Actar 911 resuscitation dummies.

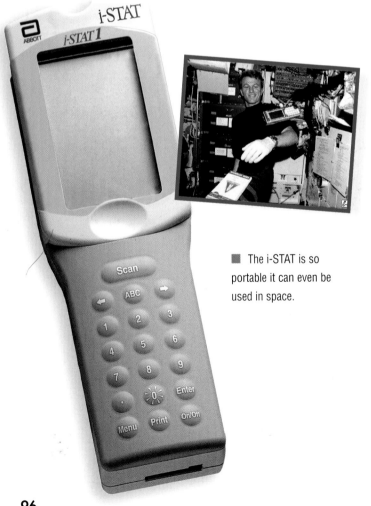

■ The i-STAT is so portable it can even be used in space.

Testing Blood in Seconds

Blood tests are done all the time—during a medical checkup, to diagnose symptoms, to monitor how well a patient's therapy is going, during a medical procedure. Usually, the sooner the results are available, the better. That's one reason why Imant Lauks, of Ontario, invented the i-STAT blood-analysis device. This small unit, which hit the marketplace in 1992, can test blood in only two minutes. And it's portable, which means that patients being moved can be tested on the go. In addition, only a small amount of blood is needed for a test, which is particularly helpful when the patient is a tiny baby. As well as being used in hundreds of hospitals, the i-STAT has already been into space, helping monitor the health of NASA astronauts.

FROGS ON A SCREEN

Doctors certainly need to learn about human anatomy, but even people who don't see a future for themselves in medicine benefit from an understanding of the parts of the body. That's why many high-school students take courses that teach them about anatomy and dissection. But cutting up a real frog? Simon Clark, of Ontario, really believed that there had to be an alternative way to learn, so he and a friend, Charles Gervais, invented the Digital Frog in 1995.

"We had lots of long days and late nights, but we ended up with something that was really cool," says Clark. Digital Frog was a CD-ROM that let students practise dissection and learn about anatomy and ecology by looking at extremely detailed full-colour pictures and text. The award-winning CD-ROM was such a big hit in North American high schools that Digital Frog 2, a new enhanced version, was produced to replace it in 1998. Animations let students see things they wouldn't be able to see with a real frog, such as blood pumping through the heart, and they can even build up and move joints. And by the way, Digital Frog continues to protect the frog population, "saving a few frogs from the scalpel," as Clark puts it.

Heart

Introduction...
The heart is the main "pump" for the frog's circulatory system, receiving blood from the veins and forcing it out through the aorta with rhythmic contractions.

The heart pumps blood twice as it makes a complete circuit through the body:

· once to force it to the lungs and the skin

· once to force it through the rest of the body.

Structure...

Function...

Arteries   Cardiac Muscle

Compare 2, 3, and 4 Chambered Hearts   ■ Stop blood flow

Pseudacris crucifer

Spring Peepers live in just about any shallow water, including marshes, swamps, ponds and ditches. Their distinctive high-pitched call can be heard over great distances. These small frogs vary in size from 1.8 cm (0.75") to 3.3 cm (1.25").

■ Digital Frog protects real frogs, as well as squeamish students by allowing digital dissection.

THREE STEPS

They look like a pair of glasses, but if you put them on properly and listen closely, they may just talk to you! In fact, that's the whole point. Ziggy (Xing) Zeng, of Montreal, got the idea in 1996, when she was thirteen. "If we have the technology to send Neil Armstrong on a moon walk, why can't we use our technology to help the visually impaired walk around on earth with ease?" she wondered. Two years later, she built some prototype talking glasses for a science fair. Instead of lenses, her glasses have ultrasonic transducers that send out ultrasonic waves, much as bats do. When they hit something, these waves get bounced back.

"The device that I've made measures the time it takes for the waves to go to and back from the object, and it calculates the distance between the user and the object," Zeng says. The glasses are adaptable to the user, and each comes with an earpiece. "The glasses convert the distance into the number of steps, according to the user's length of stride, and it tells them this distance in a human voice." Zeng has applied for a patent for her prize-winning invention.

■ Ziggy Zeng's talking glasses use a form of echolocation to make life easier for the visually impaired.

COMING THROUGH IN A CRUTCH

When his stepmother broke her leg in a snowmobiling accident and was forced to move about using crutches, twelve-year-old Justin Anis got his brainwave. "I realized how big an inconvenience this can be. Some of life's easiest tasks were made a lot more difficult."

That's why he and a friend, Tyler Mitchell, invented Comfy Crutches in 2000. Regular crutches are made "comfy" with the addition of carry pouches, drink holders, a back-scratcher, a fan, and even shoes for extra traction!

"There is a little Velcro attached to each feature so you can organize the items wherever it is easiest for you to reach," explains Justin. "We also provide some additional Velcro so you can stick some onto something we don't provide, like a cellphone, and stick that on your crutches."

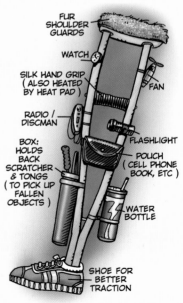

FUR SHOULDER GUARDS

WATCH

SILK HAND GRIP (ALSO HEATED BY HEAT PAD)

FAN

RADIO / DISCMAN

FLASHLIGHT

BOX: HOLDS BACK SCRATCHER & TONGS (TO PICK UP FALLEN OBJECTS)

POUCH (CELL PHONE BOOK, ETC)

WATER BOTTLE

SHOE FOR BETTER TRACTION

Bits and Pieces

A Mixed Bag of Inventions

Yes, this is the place where you can find inventions that just don't seem to fit into the other categories. Of course, there wasn't room to include *every* Canadian invention. Some had to be left out—including the elastic training aids developed by the owners of nine German shepherds to reduce dog-barking; the virtual reality mouse that helps blind computer users "feel" objects; and the computer software Kyle Doerksen invented to incorporate 3D imaging into existing ground-penetrating radar, which will help detect buried land mines.

But there's still lots here to dazzle you, from a new kind of rake to a new way of organizing time. Enjoy!

Take Your Time

Just over one hundred years ago, there was no standard time. This meant that you set your clocks by the position of the sun in the sky. It also meant that almost every community in Canada had its clocks set to a different time. Your clock might read 4:05, while the clock of a friend in a neighbouring town might read 3:51. You can imagine how annoying this would be if you were trying to plan a train schedule!

In fact, it was the railway companies in North America that first began following the plan suggested by Sir Sandford Fleming. In 1878, this Scottish-born Canadian proposed dividing the globe into twenty-four equal time zones, one for each hour of the day. Because the earth spins 360 degrees in one day, it travels 15 degrees in each hour. Each zone would cover 15 degrees in longitude, and all places within a time zone would have the same time. This meant that when it was noon where you live, it would be one hour later in a place 15 degrees east of you and one hour earlier in a place 15 degrees west of you.

In 1883, Canada adopted standard time, and by the end of the nineteenth century, almost all the countries in the world were following it as well. Canada was divided into seven time zones, but eventually the Yukon Territories opted to join with Pacific time, meaning Canada now has six time zones. So next time you want to phone your friend in Whitehorse from Charlottetown at seven in the morning, you can do the calculation … and then stop dialling! (It would be three in the morning in the Yukon then. Yawn!)

■ Because of Sir Sandford Fleming (below), the world now operates on a standardized timetable. The globe at left shows how Fleming divided the earth into twenty-four different zones.

ZIIIIIIIPPPPP!

Who invented the zipper? Was it really an American, as some claim, or was it a Canadian? According to Wayne Grady, in *Chasing the Chinook*, it seems that in 1896, an American inventor, Whitcomb Judson, invented something very zipper-like. Then in 1913, Gideon Sundback, a Swedish-born inventor working in the United States, patented an invention, a separable fastener, which also seemed very zipper-like. An American company patented a similar fastener, called the Talon Slide Fastener, in 1917.

Sundback became president of the Lightning Fastener Company of St. Catharines, Ontario, in 1925. He received the Canadian patent for his separable fasteners, which he now called Lightning Fasteners. His company began manufacturing and selling them to the B. F. Goodrich Company, which replaced the hook-and-eye fasteners on its rubber galoshes with these fasteners, and then called the boots Zippers. As you may have guessed, this soon became the name of the fastener too!

That's a complicated story. But now you can make up your own mind. Are zippers a Canadian invention or not?

ROLL 'EM

Norman Breakey, of Toronto, invented the paint roller in 1940. Who could paint a ceiling without it?

CAMERA CRAZY

The world's first panoramic camera (which could take a picture in a complete circle with one exposure) was patented by John Connon in 1887 in Elora, Ontario. In 1934, a patent for the first modern television camera was obtained by F. C. P. Henroteau, of Ottawa.

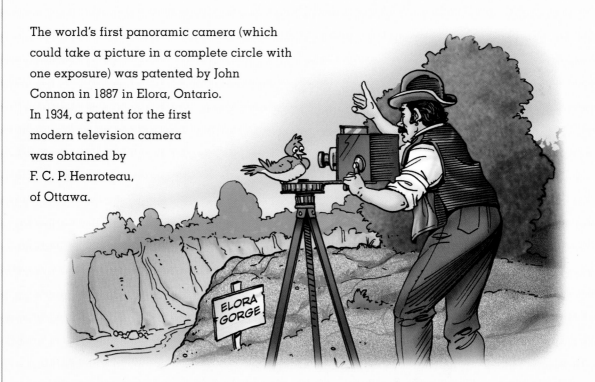

THE COLOUR OF GREEN

When the family canning factory in Winnipeg went out of business in the mid-1940s, Harry Wasylyk began a new venture. He started making bags from a new product called polyethylene and selling them to stores. The bags, he believed, could be used for packaging fruits and vegetables. He also began making surgical gloves from polyethylene and selling them to the Winnipeg General Hospital.

It wasn't long before the staff at the hospital began complaining to him about how difficult it was to keep their garbage cans clean. Wasylyk invented something to solve that problem: green garbage bags to line the cans! Eventually, people began using them to put out household garbage too.

■ This sheet of polyethylene is ready to be made into garbage bags.

KEEPING AN EYE ON YOU

Sometimes people lose an eye as the result of a disease or an accident. Although their vision can not be replaced using existing technologies, they can choose to substitute an artificial eye for the missing one. Traditionally, any such replacement eye wasn't able to blink or move. But in 2000, that all changed.

An engineering team at the University of Alberta created a robotic eye linked to the world's tiniest electrical motor. Why? Dr. Max Meng, director of the university's advanced robotics and teleoperation lab, explains, "This robotic prosthetic eye is the first one in the world that moves in sync with the natural eye, using human brain signals."

As the patient's brain sends electronic signals to his natural eye, electrodes placed on both sides of his head pick up the same information and pass it on to the robotic eye. The information is then interpreted, and the eye moves accordingly. Dr. Meng adds, "It looks completely natural. You wouldn't be able to tell the difference between a real eye and this one."

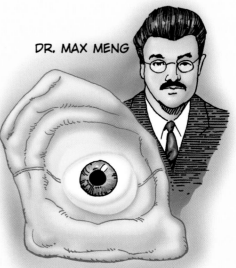

DR. MAX MENG

ROBOTIC PROSTHETIC EYE

MAKING CONNECTIONS

When the Royal Canadian Air Force asked for help designing and manufacturing structures for aircraft hangars to be built in the Arctic, Art Fentiman decided to lend a hand. He studied the requirements: the structure had to be made of lightweight, compact materials, and it had to be easy to put together and take down using simple tools. It would be covered in canvas, plastic, or fibreglass panels. That's how Fentiman invented the Triodetic system of construction.

Fentiman designed aluminum or steel tubes with special ends that could be fit into an aluminum hub with toothed slots. A bolt was tightened to hold everything in place. It could be covered in various types of materials. The concept was simple but brilliant. Now it is used in buildings around the world, from schools to hockey arenas to playground jungle gyms!

■ The Triodetic system is so lightweight and practical that it's now be used in construction projects all over the world.

GIVE ME A HAND

In 1945, Eric Leaver had a great idea. Although it seemed like science fiction at the time, he wanted to build a type of machine tool that could work automatically at a task. The machine would have a "hand" and an "arm," so it could reproduce the movements that a human hand and arm can make, only it would be much, much stronger.

A Canadian engineer, George Mounce, helped Leaver develop the prototype, and by 1947 people around the world were coming to a factory in Toronto to watch just such a tool in action. Leaver had invented a hand-arm machine that could be programmed to automatically make a simple part. He and Mounce received the patent for the machine in 1949, and later sold licences to two American companies, General Electric and Giddings and Lewis.

"Today I get a thrill every time I visit a modern automobile assembly plant and look down on the forest of 'robots' spot-welding the bodies," says Leaver, "for they aren't really robots—they are in fact hand-arm machines! And interestingly, they are still using electronic controls."

■ Eric Leaver's hand-arm machine made possible many of today's "robot" workers.

■ Hugh Le Caine demonstrates the electronic Sackbutt, much to the amusement of the Duke of Edinburgh (far right).

Music Plugged In

He had invented his first musical instrument by the time he was four, was giving public piano recitals when he was six, and loved electronics. Put these together and you get Hugh Le Caine, of Thunder Bay, Ontario. In 1945, Le Caine invented the world's first voltage-controlled music synthesizer, the electronic Sackbutt. He also invented the touch-sensitive keyboard and a variable-speed multi-track tape recorder. He even produced an electronic musical piece called "Dripsody" by electronically manipulating the sound of a single drop of water. Have a listen sometime!

More recently, another guy with a love of music and electronics, seventeen-year-old Michael Neufeld, of Kelowna, B.C., has combined his interests and invented the award-winning Music without Media MP3 player. This computer-independent audio player can store huge amounts of music—more than one hundred hours (which is ninety-eight hours more than commercially available players can handle) on an ordinary PC hard drive. Then the tunes can be played back and enjoyed on a stereo … for a loooooooong time!

Neufeld says: "I designed the player because I enjoy a variety of music. Whether I want to listen to the Rolling Stones or Mozart, U2 or the Barenaked Ladies—they're all just the press of a button away, in my car, home, or anywhere else!"

JUST GOTTA BOUNCE

Olivia Poole grew up on the White Earth Indian Reservation in Minnesota. She recalled seeing happy babies strapped to thin boards called cradleboards and suspended by long leather thongs from bendy tree branches. The babies' feet touched the ground, and they would bounce up and down at will. In the early 1950s, Poole decided to try to recreate this contraption to entertain her youngest child. Combining the new with the old, she invented the first prototype of the Jolly Jumper, using a broom handle as a crosspiece, a coiled spring, and a fabric harness. The adjustable jumper was attached in a doorway.

In the late 1950s, Poole and her husband moved to British Columbia, where they began manufacturing and selling Jolly Jumpers. The product was a bouncing success, and was soon being sold all over North America, Australia, and Britain.

■ Jolly Jumpers have been keeping babies happy for almost fifty years.

JUST PICTURE IT

When the city of Montreal hosted Expo 67, people flocked to the fair from all around the world. Not all of them spoke English—and yet, when they needed to use the washrooms, they could easily figure out which was for women and which for men. How was this achieved? With the help of Paul Arthur. At Expo 67, Arthur introduced his revolutionary method of communication: the pictograph. The symbols he invented, one for the women's washroom door and one for the men's, helped visitors to the fair instantly identify which restroom was which.

From there, Arthur's idea quickly grew. In 1968, he began creating a whole universal language based on three shapes: a triangle warns of danger, a circle shows what is prohibited or allowed, and a square gives information. Arthur worked on his system for almost thirty years. Now it includes more than 450 clear and understandable "pictos," or symbols.

Arthur also realized that there is a difference between simply putting up signs and actually helping people find their way by taking into account more of their needs (called "wayfinding"). Arthur thought of wayfinding as a two-step process, consisting of "decision making" (determining where you want to go) and "decision executing" (figuring out how to get there). It involves looking at the activity, behaviour, and abilities of humans to determine how signs, street numbers, and other directional aids should be designed and where they should be placed.

Paul Arthur understood that wayfinding systems could help all people—especially the elderly, the disabled, and those unable to read—find their way without difficulty on city streets, inside large hospitals and airports, and even on bus and subway systems.

■ Instead of lifting after every raking motion, you can simply roll this handy rake on wheels into place, thanks to the Quesnelles.

RAKING IT IN

When you have a sore arm, raking leaves can be difficult. This problem was all it took to spur on Stella Quesnelle and her husband, Albert, to invent a rake on wheels! The Lawn Star Rake rolls along easily when it's pushed. And when it's pulled back, the teeth flip down and lock into place. Let the raking begin!

KNOCK, KNOCK

Wait! Just because Jeremy Cooperstock isn't in his office at McGill University in Montreal doesn't mean there's no one there. Say hello to his invention, the Automated Door Attendant (ADA), and it just may say hello back.

Cooperstock invented the ADA when he realized that it was difficult for his students to schedule time to meet with him. The ADA helps with scheduling and gives students information about the professor and his areas of interest. When a student steps in front of the door, a motion detector senses it and a menu pops up on a screen, prompting the student to say a command. The student's voice activates another set of options, and these allow him or her to leave a message, schedule an appointment, or view finished projects done by the professor.

■ Jeremy Cooperstock's ADA is a personal assistant with a twist.

THIN FILM

Take a look at the Canadian twenty-dollar bill—or the fifty-dollar bill, or the hundred-dollar bill. See that ultra-thin gold-coloured patch up in the left-hand corner? It's an optical security device, and it's made up of several layers of ceramic material. Turn the bill at an angle and you'll see the gold turn green. That's how you can tell if the bill is real or counterfeit. Only a real optical security device on a real bill will turn green. It takes sophisticated equipment to create this patch, and it's almost impossible to reproduce it. So you just might say that since 1989, when the foil first began to be added to Canadian bills over twenty dollars, counterfeiters have been foiled by this Canadian invention!

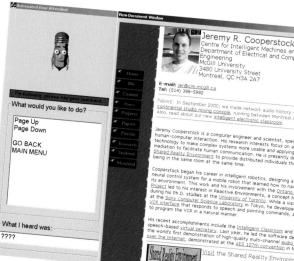

■ Ordinary tennis balls mean fewer distractions for the students and the teacher.

KEEPING QUIET

One day, Margaret Woolfrey and Patricia Bilyk began cutting holes in old tennis balls and sticking them on the bottoms of chair legs. Why? These two Canadian speech-language pathologists had heard of others doing this to reduce the noise in their classrooms so that students had fewer distractions. "The noise level of a single chair scraping across a floor can be just less than that of a jackhammer or a motorcycle. It's very loud!" says Woolfrey. So they thought they would give the tennis balls a try—and they worked.

But it was hard to get enough used tennis balls, and cutting the holes in them was difficult and dangerous. "It was a horrendous task," Woolfrey remembers. "I did one classroom set and cut myself, and I decided never to do it again."

So in 1997, the two women put their heads together and decided to find a way around this obstacle. "We wondered if we should just start our own company and offer these as a ready-made product," recalls Woolfrey. That's just what they did. Now their company, Sound Listening, manufactures felt-covered balls with a precision cut so they fit perfectly on the bottom of chair legs—and no one gets hurt making them any more!

FOG CATCHER

Ever heard of fog catchers? Well, they exist—thanks to Robert Schemenauer and his team from Environment Canada, who successfully invented them in 1992. What do fog catchers do? Well, they catch fog, obviously. What may not be so obvious is what happens next. The fog catchers, set up on the mountains of El Tofo, Chile, turn the fog into drinkable water, which is then shipped in pipes to waterless regions many kilometres away. Now that's an invention that turns the taps on!

■ Robert Schemenauer's fog catchers at work.

WHEN YOU GOTTA GO

Is the toilet a perfect invention? Some Canadians think it could be improved. That's why, in 1994, James Pendlebury invented a special device that automatically closes the lid after the toilet is flushed. Never again will that seat be up at the wrong time! And have a look at the Flusher 2000. In 1999, five Grade 5 friends in Georgetown, Ontario, created this very, very comfortable toilet for a science fair. It has a pile-covered headrest, armrests, and even a padded seat. An attached table is a perfect spot for resting magazines— or even a television. And to top it all off, there is an automatic cranking device that makes sure you get just the right amount of toilet paper. Now that's comfort.

TOASTY TOES

What do you do with wet boots when you come in from making a snow fort or playing hockey? Throw them in a heap on the hall floor, where they may take days to dry, right? Well, that's what Colette Laferrière's children used to do. Then the Sainte-Foy, Quebec, mom took action. She invented (hold onto your soggy hat!) an electric boot-dryer. It even has a thermostat and a timer, so the boots don't get overheated! Now when Laferrière's kids go to whip on their boots for another plunge into the snowbanks, their footwear is dry and ready.

KEEPING WHAT'S UP TOP WARM

ALOUETTE!

Have you ever worn a toque? It's that knitted cap that looks a bit like a stocking with a tassel on the end. It was invented in the 1600s in New France (which was part of what is now Quebec), became popular, and now is worn on many heads across Canada every winter. In fact, even Bonhomme, the jovial snowman who hosts the Quebec Winter Carnival every year, wears one to keep that round head warm!

Acknowledgements

For their considerable contributions to this project, I would like to offer my particular thanks to Catherine Betz, National Research Council; Antony Pacey, National Museum of Science and Technology Corporation; Dr. Robert Park, University of Waterloo; and Rachel Zimmerman, Canadian Space Agency.

I would also like to show my appreciation for the help, which was given with such goodwill, of the following people: William Abbott; Fred Addis, the Pier; Nancy Ames, Cereal Research Centre; Richard Anderson, Canadian Agriculture Library; Justin Anis; Ian Anthony, Rogers Communications; David Aung; Susan Best, Hutchison House; Kim Blank, University of Victoria; Randy Buhler; Tim Bray; Blissymbolics Communications International; Bob Bryniak; Jeremy Cooperstock, McGill University; Julie Cöuet, Canadian Space Agency; Dianne Croteau; James De Laurier; Lynn Delgaty, National Research Council; Denis Désilets; Jennifer DuBois, Mathis Instruments; Charlie Embree, Agriculture and Agri-Food Canada; Lily and Martin Erlic; Ron Fentiman; Lise Gagne, Environment Canada; Ken and Gina Gallant; David Garrison, Yes magazine; Matthew Garvin; Gino Gemma; James Gosling; Alan G. Hobbs; William Humber; Andrew Jamieson, Atlantic Food and Horticulture Research Centre; William Kay, University of Victoria; Ann-Marie Kelleher, Lang Pioneer Village; Wayne Kelly; Shahrokh Khanizadeh, Agriculture and Agri-Food Canada; Louise Kinross, Bloorview Macmillan; Judith Knudsen; Angela Kypreos, Hospital for Sick Children; Michael Lachapelle, Canadian Lacrosse Association; Eric Leaver; Max Meng, University of Calgary; Anie Miner; Michel Monette, Musée de la civilisation; Wendy Murphy; Benno Nigg, University of Calgary; Jack and Mark Nowinski; Pat Orr, Ganong Brothers; Danielle Parney; Stella Quesnelle; Graham Quirk; Debby Roman, Ballard Power Systems; Inge Russell; John Scott; Susan Scott; Randall Sherwood; Mario Theriault; Dr. Larry Wang; Robert Wilson, Environment Canada; the Women Inventors Project; Margaret Woolfrey; David Zakutin; and Ziggy Zeng.

Photo credits

Care has been taken to trace ownership of copyright materials contained in this book. Information enabling the publisher to rectify any reference or credit line in future editions will be welcomed.

Page 4 (middle), 60: courtesy Gino Gemma; 4 (bottom right), 33 (top left): Hockey Hall of Fame; 4 (bottom left), 33 (top right): Dave Sandford/Hockey Hall of Fame; 5 (top), 52: courtesy Steve Mann; 5 (bottom), 46 (top): Creed and Co.; 6 (from top to bottom): Bombardier Inc.; Nova Scotia Archives and Records; Basketball Hall of Fame, Springfield, MA; courtesy of the N. C. Division of Archives and History; from the collections of Henry Ford Museum and Greenfield Village; Canada Aviation Museum; Vic Thompson/W. Murphy Enterprises; 6 (bottom), 46 (bottom): courtesy of Rogers Comnications Inc.; 7 (top): from the collections of Henry Ford Museum and Greenfield Village; 7 (middle right): Robert Flaherty/NAC/PA-143593; 7 (middle left), 98: Pierre Paul Poulin/Magma; 7 (bottom), 53: John Tamblyn; 8 (top), 58: Parks Canada/Alexander Graham Bell National Historic Site of Canada; 8 (bottom), 93: Fraser Shein; 9, 12 (bottom): Richard Harrington/NAC/PA-129935; 10 (top): Richard Harrington/NAC/PA-129937; 10 (bottom): Richard Harrington/NAC/PA-114660; 11: Richard Harrington/NAC/PA-129886; 12 (from top to bottom): NAC/PA-122730, NAC/C-003805, NAC/C-003806; 13: Richard Harrington/NAC/

PA-143237; 14 (top): NAC/PA-194326; 14 (inset): Draper & Co. & C. L. Andrews/NAC/PA-022449; 15 (top): Ville de Montréal, Gestion de documents et archives; 15 (bottom): National Research Council Canada; 16, 17: Bombardier Inc.; 18: National Research Council Canada; 19: Campbell Scientific (Canada) Corp.; 20: Norquest Innovation Corp. (www.polardome.com); 21, 27: courtesy Brown Brothers; 23 (top): NAC/C-053499; 23 (bottom): NAC/C-053503; 24: courtesy Labatt Brewing Co. Ltd.; 25: Ballard Power Systems; 26: Nova Scotia Archives and Records; 28: courtesy of the Manning Innovation Awards; 29 (top): Keith Minchin–Photographer– Faces of Fredericton; 29 (bottom): Conserval Engineering, Inc.; 30: University of Ottawa; 31: James Inglis/NAC/C-001959; 32: H. J. Woodside/NAC/PA-016239; 33 (top left): Hockey Hall of Fame; 33 (top right): Dave Sandford/Hockey Hall of Fame; 33 (bottom): NAC/PA-164629; 34: Patent and Copyright Office/NAC/C-005567; 35: courtesy Wayne Kelly; 36: courtesy Canada's Sports Hall of Fame; 37: Steve Ward/Hockey Hall of Fame; 38, 39: Basketball Hall of Fame, Springfield, MA; 40: courtesy Horn Abbot Ltd.; 41: courtesy Wrebbit Inc.; 42: courtesy Sheryl Nadler; 43: NAC/PA-092361; 44: NAC/C-023568; 45: NAC/C-014483; 47: CP Wirephoto/NAC/PA-141575; 48: courtesy of the Canadian Space Agency (www.space.gc.ca); 49: courtesy of IMAX Corporation; 50, 51: courtesy of the N. C. Division of Archives and History; 55: Frances Ann Hopkins/NAC/C-016425; 56 (top): NAC/PA-074670; 56 (middle): Robert Flaherty/NAC/PA-113955; 56 (bottom): A. P. Low/NAC/PA-051464; 57 (top): NAC/PA-124109; 57 (bottom): NAC/PA-124109; 59: Eric Robbins/North American Laser Class; 62: from the collections of Henry Ford Museum & Greenfield Village; 63: courtesy U.S. Patent and Trademark Office; 64: NAC/C-020603; 65 (top): NAC/C-009772; 65 (bottom): Jiger Corp.; 66: courtesy Gina Gallant; 67: NAC/PA-124197; 68 (top): NAC/PA-124196; 68 (bottom): Stephen Greenlees/NAC/PA-151365; 69 (top); NAC/PA-063923; 69 (bottom): National Research Council Canada; 70: photo by Hugh Mackechnie (Avro Aircraft), courtesy of David Mackechnie; 72, 73 (top): Canada Aviation Museum; 73 (bottom): National Research Council Canada; 74: courtesy of the Canadian Space Agency (www.space.gc.ca); 75: National Research Council Canada; 76: courtesy Project Ornithopter Inc.; 77: Fulton's Pancake House and Sugar Bush; 78: courtesy Dr. Larry Wang; 79: courtesy Nova Scotia Fruit Growers Association; 80: courtesy Andrew Jamieson; 81: courtesy of Agriculture and Agri-Food Canada; 82: NAC/PA-211610; 83: Canola Council Canada; 84 (top): NAC/PA-0492110; 84 (bottom), 85: Fulton's Pancake House and Sugar Bush; 86: Robert Teteruek; 87: courtesy of Agriculture and Agri-Food Canada; 88: Howard Dill Enterprises; 89, 94 (bottom): Tom Sandler/W. Murphy Enterprises; 90: Geza Karpathi/NAC/C-067451; 91: National Research Council Canada; 92 (top): courtesy Jack and Mark Nowinski; 92 (bottom): courtesy Dr. Thomas Ming Swi Chang; 93: Fraser Shein; 94 (top): Vic Thompson/W. Murphy Enterprises; 95: John Comber/W. Murphy Enterprises; 95 (inset): Myrna Maxwell/W. Murphy Enterprises; 96 (top): courtesy Studio Innova; 96 (bottom): courtesy i-STAT Corporation; 97: Digital Frog International; 99: courtesy Dr. Robert Schemenauer; 100 (left): R. Matthews, Anderson & Chapman/NAC/C-001166; 100 (right): NAC/C-014128; 102: Chris Close/The Image Bank; 103 (top): Christine Fentiman/Triodetic; 103 (bottom): Fortune magazine, 1946; 104: NAC/PA-167153; 105: Jolly Jumper; 106 (top): courtesy Stella Quesnelle/Royal Bank Reporter; 106 (bottom): Marisa Wyse and David Bancroft; 107: Sound Listening Environments Inc.; 108: courtesy Dr. Robert Schemenauer.

INDEX

Page numbers in italics refer to photographs or illustrations.

Abbott, Scott, 40
acetylene gas, 23
Actar 911, 96, *96*
Ahearn, Thomas, 65, *65*
Al-Temen, Ihsan, 93
Allen, Steve, *65*
Alouette satellite, 48, 75
Ames, Nancy, 88
Anik satellite, 48, *48*, 49
Anis, Justin, 98
anti-gravity flight suit, 69, *69*
apple cultivars, 79
Arthur, Paul, 105
artificial blood cell, 92
Asselbergs, Edward, 87
Aung, David, 83
Automated Door Attendant (ADA), 106, *106*
Avro Arrow, 70–71, *70*
Baldwin, Casey, 58
Ball of Dreams, 71, *71*
Ballard, Geoff, 25
Banting, Frederick, 5
barley tortilla, 88
baseball, 41, *41*
basketball, 38–39, *38, 39*
batteryless radio, 47
Beaudoin, Jim, 15, *15*
Beaver airplane, 68, *68*
Beers, William, 34
Bell, Alexander Graham, 7, 45, *45*, 51, 58
Benedict, Clint, 33, *33*
Best, Charles, 5
Bethune, Norman, 90, *90*
Bethune rib shears, 90
bicycle helmet, 66, *66*
Bigelow, Wilfrid, 91
Bilyk, Patricia, 107
Biodiesel fuel, 24
Blanchard, Pierre, 37
Blank, Kim, 82
Blissymbol Printer, 53, *53*
bola, 10
Bombardier, Joseph-Armand, *6, 7*, 16–17, *16*
Bombardier, Léopold, 16
Boocock, David, 24
Brault, Richard, 96
Bray, Tim, 54
Breakey, Norman, 101
Brown, Alan, 86
Brown, Paul, 30, *30*
Bruce, Ian, 59

Bryniak, Bob, 66
Buhler, Randy, 20
Cabot strawberry, 80, *80*
calcium carbide, 23
Canadarm, 74, *74*, 75
canoe, 55, 56, *56*
canola, 83, *83*
Cartwright, Alexander, 41
Chang, Thomas Ming Swi, 92, *92*
Clark, Simon, 97
Cold Buster bar, 78, *78*
Collings, Tim, 52
Comfy Crutches, 98, *98*
concrete toboggan, *10*, 11, *11*
conductive concrete, 15, *15*
Conklin, Dak, 60
Connon, John, 101
Cooperstock, Jeremy, 106
Crash Position Indicator (CPI), 69, *69*
Creed, Frederick, 46
crokinole, 35, *35*
Croteau, Dianne, 96
Danisch, Lee, 75
Deep Rover submersible, 60
Deep Worker 2000, 60, 61
DeLaurier, James, 76
Désilets, Denis, 85
digital acoustic imaging system (Daisy), 61, *61*
Digital Frog, 97, *97*
Dill, Howard, 88, *88*
Doerksen, Kyle, 99
Doubleday, Abner, 41
Drake, Theodore, 86
edible cup, 83, *83*
Edison, Thomas, 22, 50
electric boot-dryer, 109
electronic Sackbutt, 104, *104*
Elliott, J. W., 14
Emery, Les, 66
Ensor, George, 82
Erlic, Martin, 86
Evans, Matthew, 22
extensible markup language (XML), 54
EyeTap, 52
Fenerty, Charles, 44
Fentiman, Art, 103
Ferguson, Graeme, 49
Fessenden, Reginald, *6*, 50–51, *50*
Fife, David, 81
Fife, Jane, 81
five-pin bowling, 35, *35*
Fleming, Sandford, 100, *100*
Flusher 2000, 108, *108*
fog catcher, 99, 108, *108*
Fogh, Hans, 59
Forbes, John, 33
Foulis, Robert, 44, *44*

Franks, Wilbur, 69, *69*, 94
frozen fish, 78
Galipeau, Anie, 30, *30*
Gallant, Gina, 7, 66, *66*
Gallant, Paul, 41
Ganong, Arthur, 82
Garvin, Matthew, 59
Gemma, Gino, 60
Gervais, Charles, 97
Gesner, Abraham, *6*, 26–27, *26*
goalie mask, 4, 33, *33*
Goodison, Barry, 19
Gosling, James, 54, *54*
Gower, John, 65
Grady, Wayne, 101
Green Walkman, 30, *30*
Griffith, T. R., 18
Guillet, James, 28
hand-arm machine, 103, *103*
Haney, Chris, 40
heart-assist device, 91
heart pacemaker, 91
Henroteau, F. C. P., 101
Heyn, Chris, 28, *28*
high-tech shoe, 42
hockey, 32, *32*, 33, 34
hockey net, 34
hockey stick, 32, 32
Hollick, John, 29
Hopps, John, 91, *91*
Humber, Bill, 41
Huntsman, Archibald, 78
Husain, Ken, 53
hydrofoil, 8, 58, *58*
ice skate, 33, 34
ice-creeper, 10
igloo, 9, 12, *12*, 13, 20
IMAX, 49, *49*
ION system, 53
i-STAT blood-analysis device, 89, 96, *96*
Jamieson, Andrew, 80, *80*
Java programming language, 54
Jiger all-terrain vehicle (ATV), 65
Johnston, Gary, 87
Jolly Jumper, 105, *105*
Judson, Whitcomb, 101
Jull, Orange, 14
Kay, William, 87
kayak, 55, 56, *56*
Kelly, Wayne, 35, 35
kerosene, 21, 26, 27
Kerr, Robert, 49
Khanizadeh, Shahrokh, 79
Kirby, Bruce, 59
Klein, George, 75, *75*
Knapp, Frederick, 57
Knudsen, Donald, 61
komatik, 10, *10*, 11

111

Kroitor, Roman, 49
lacrosse, 31, 34, *34*
Laferrière, Colette, 109
Laser sailboat, 59, *59*
Lauks, Imant, 96
Lawn Star Rake, 106, *106*
Le Caine, Hugh, 104, *104*
Leaver, Eric, 103
light bulb, 22, *22*
Lind, Kaare, 93
Lishman, Bill, 76
Lubricator Cup, 7, *62*, 63
Mackie, Cameron, 64
Mann, Steve, 5, 52, *52*
maple syrup, 84–85
Marconi, Guglielmo, 50-51
Marquis wheat, 81, *81*
matches, 26–27
Mathis, Nancy, 29, *29*
McCoy, Elijah, *6*, 62–63, *62*
McCoy, Emillia, 62
McCoy, George, 62
McIntosh apple, 79, *79*
McIntosh, John, 79
McLaurin, Colin, 93
Meng, Max, 102
Metcalfe, John, 19
Misra, Santosh, 87
Mitchell, Tyler, 98
mobile blood service, 90, *90*
mobile medical unit, 90
Morse keyboard perforator, 5, 46, *46*
Mounce, George, 103
Munro, Donald, 37
Murphy, Wendy, 6, 94–95, *94*, *95*
Music without Media MP3 player, 104
Mussivand, Tofy, 91
myoelectric hand, 8, 93, *93*
MyoMicro, 93, *93*
Naismith, James, 6, 38–39, *38*
Nanaimo bar, 82
Neufeld, Michael, 104
newsprint, 44
Newtsuit, 61, *61*
Nigg, Benno, 42
Noorduyn Norseman, 68, *68*, 71
Noorduyn, Robert, 68
Nowinski, Barbara, 92
Nowinski, Jack, 92
Nowinski, Mark, 92
Nuytten, Phil, 60, 61
optical security device, 106, *106*
ornithopter, 76, *76*
Orr, John, 18
Pablum, 86, *86*
paint roller, 101, *101*
panoramic camera, 101, *101*
Patch, John, 57, *57*

patent, 28, *28*
PEM fuel cell, 25, *25*
Pendlebury, James, 108
personal electrocardiograph, 92, *92*
Peters, Aganetta, 87
pictograph, 105, *105*
Ping Gu, 15
Ping Xie, 15
Pisces submarine, 4, 60, *60*-61
Plante, Jacques, 33
plastic gas, 28
polyethylene, 102, *102*
Poole, Olivia, 105
poutine, 87
Predovich, Bob, 53
propeller de-icer, 18, *18*
Pullman, George, 64
pumpkin seeds, 88
Puvanesasingham, Ram, 28, *28*
Quesnelle, Albert, 106, *106*
Quesnelle, Stella, 106, *106*
quinzhee, 20, *20*
railway sleeper car, 64, *64*
Red Fife wheat, 81
reduced-drag boat hull, 59
Reimer, Ernie, 75
reverse polymerization, 66
robotic eye, 102, *102*
Robson, Thomas, 44
Rogers, Edward, 6, *46*, 47
Roller Boat, 57, *57*
rotary snowplow, 14, *14*
Russell, Inge, 24
Ryan, Thomas, 35
Saunders, Charles, 81, *81*
Sauter, William, 93
Schemenauer, Robert, 108
Scott, John, 53
screw propeller, 57
Seller, Peg (Margaret Shearer), 36, *36*
Sewell, Richard, 58
Sharp, Samuel, 64
shatter-free railway track, 64
Shearer, Cameron, 53
Shepody potato, 87, *87*
Sicard, Arthur, 15
Ski-Doo, 16–17, *16*, 17
Slicklicker, 58, 58
snow blower, 15, 15
snow-depth sensor, 19, *19*
snow dome, 20, *20*
snow goggles, 11, *11*
snow knife, 12
snowshoe, 7, 13, *13*
soapstone lamp, 13, *13*
Solarwall, 29, 29
speed-sensing baseball, 42, *42*
standard time, 100

steam foghorn, 44
Stefanyshyn, Darren, 42
STEM antenna, 75, *75*
Stephenson, William, 47, *47*
Stevinson, Harry, 69, *69*
stilts, 37, *37*
Sundback, Gideon, 101
super yeast, 24, *24*
table-top hockey, 37, *37*
talking glasses, 98, *98*
tarte au sucre (recipe), 85
TC Probe, 29, *29*
telephone, 45, *45*
television camera, 101
Thiessen, Alfred, 51
Thomson, Mack, 60
3D puzzle, 41, 41
Tisdall, Frederick, 86
toe-thrusting skate, 34, *34*
toque, 109, *109*
towed underwater flying craft, 60, *60*
Triodetic system, 103, *103*
Trivial Pursuit, 40, *40*
Troth, Harvey, 28
Turnbull, Wallace Rupert, 6, 72–73, *72*
umiak, 56, *56*
v-chip, 52
variable-pitch propeller, 72–73, *72*, 73
Wakeling, James, 42
Wang, Larry, 78, *78*
Wasylyk, Harry, 102
Watson, Thomas, 45
wayfinding, 105
wearable computer, 5, 52, 52
Webster, Bill, 26, 27
Webster, Harriet, 27
WEEVAC 6, 94–95, *94*, *95*
Whelpley, James, 33
Willgress, Joy, 82
Willson, Thomas, 23, *23*
Wilson, Bob, 19
wireless radio, 50–51
wireless phototography transmitter, 47, *47*
Wong, Alfred, 44
Wong, Christine, 44
Woodward, Henry, 22
Woolfrey, Margaret, 107
Wright, J. J., 65
Wright, Orville, 72
Wright, Wilbur, 72
Yan Fu, 15
Yukon Gold potato, 87
Zaks, 36, *36*
Zakutin, Dave, 42, *42*
Zeigler, James, 36
Zeng, Ziggy (Xing), 7, 98, *98*
Zimmerman, Rachel, 7, 53, *53*
zipper, 101